BIG PROFITS FROM SMALL PROPERTIES

BIG PROFITS FROM SMALL PROPERTIES

HOW TO ACHIEVE FINANCIAL INDEPENDENCE BY INVESTING IN REAL ESTATE

MICHAEL E. HEENEY

iUniverse LLC
Bloomington

Big Profits from Small Properties

HOW TO ACHIEVE FINANCIAL INDEPENDENCE BY INVESTING IN REAL ESTATE

iUniverse books may be ordered through booksellers or by contacting:

iUniverse
1663 Liberty Drive
Bloomington, IN 47403
www.iuniverse.com
1-800-Authors (1-800-288-4677)

Because of the dynamic nature of the Internet, any web addresses or links contained in this book may have changed since publication and may no longer be valid. The views expressed in this work are solely those of the author and do not necessarily reflect the views of the publisher, and the publisher hereby disclaims any responsibility for them.

Any people depicted in stock imagery provided by Thinkstock are models, and such images are being used for illustrative purposes only.

Certain stock imagery © Thinkstock.

ISBN: 978-1-4759-6111-9 (sc)
ISBN: 978-1-4759-6112-6 (hc)
ISBN: 978-1-4759-6113-3 (e)

Library of Congress Control Number: 2012921230

Printed in the United States of America

iUniverse rev. date: 06/28/2013

Contents

Acknowledgments

I would like to thank those who have made this book a reality. I must express my extreme appreciation for my editor, Jon Hueber, for his work dotting my i's and crossing my t's. Also, thank you to the people at iUniverse who made this publication possible.

My son Matthew is owed deep gratitude for his superb editorial assistance in organizing the content. Many thanks to my son Scott, who works as general manager of our property operations.

I'd like to express appreciation to my wife, Stephanie, and to my daughter, Nicole, who provided the utmost inspiration.

Disclaimer

Limit of Liability/Disclaimer of Warranty: While the publisher and author have used their best efforts in preparing this book, they make no representations or warranties with respect to the accuracy or completeness of the contents of this book and specifically disclaim any implied warranties of merchantability or fitness for a particular purpose. No warranty may be created or extended by sales representatives or written sales materials. The advice and strategies contained herein may not be suitable for your situation. The publisher is not engaged in rendering professional services, and you should consult a professional where appropriate. Neither the publisher nor author shall be liable for any loss of profit or any other commercial damages, including but not limited to special, incidental, consequential, or other damages.

Introduction

I believed in myself, and I had confidence. I knew how to do it, had natural talent and I pursued it.

—*Muhammad Ali, boxer*

While foreclosures and unemployment dominate today's headlines, enterprising investors are taking advantage of a great buyer's market for just about any type of real estate. Today's property and mortgage markets offer up some of the most advantageous opportunities of any time in the recent past. This is one of the best times in recent history to implement a real estate investment strategy.

My long love affair with real estate began when my wife and I purchased our first home. After making modest improvements over the first year of ownership, we refinanced the property and netted $15,000. That amount was about 40 percent of the annual salary I was earning from working as a salesman for a consumer products company. I thought to myself, "Well, how long has this been going on?"

Over the next several years I bought and sold many small homes and apartment houses as a part-time endeavor. When I first started, my goal was similar to that of many owners in residential real estate. I collected the rents and tried hard not to spend any money on the properties. This strategy produced a below-average collection record, consistent vacancies, and many requests for maintenance. So my earlier experiences in real estate

1

were characterized by periods of trial and error. I made just about every mistake you can imagine. After lots of experimentation, I finally achieved financial independence through the specific strategies described in this book. After considering the elements that led to my success, I have detailed clearly expressed fundamentals for finding income property, financing your acquisitions, and managing your investments to obtain maximum income from your properties.

This book will enlighten you about what is involved in income property ownership and investment. If you have imagination, energy, and lots of persistence, the field of real estate is chock full of opportunities. A by-product of obtaining an independent income is that your net worth can balloon rapidly. Under most operations a net worth of $1 million will create a 10 percent annual return of approximately $100,000, a worthwhile initial goal. This book offers readers an example of how anyone starting with a very small amount of capital can create his or her own financial independence and a net worth of whatever is desired.

The book will show you how to

- invest small amounts of money and time in real estate to obtain a modest level of financial security, and
- build a six- to seven-figure net worth through continuous use of its fundamentals for real estate investment.

Now is the best time to start. As a result of the financial crisis, overall real estate prices are equivalent to what they were several years ago. Interest rates today are at their lowest levels since the 1950s. Rental property demand from tenants is increasing as migration and population trends continue their upward trajectory.

Foreclosures are way up, while mortgage approvals are down. Since the housing market tanked, home ownership has given way to home renting. The number of renters in the United States alone swelled by 3.9 million between 2004 and 2010, according to Harvard University's Joint Center for Housing Studies. In a nutshell, about 38 million households are now renters. Increased demand for rental housing has lowered the nationwide vacancy factor, which is good news for owners of rental property.

As we learn from *The Millionaire Next Door* by Thomas J. Stanley, PhD and William D. Danko, PhD, 80 percent of American millionaires are first-generation millionaires: ordinary people who have accumulated their wealth in one generation. When principal residence, or home equity, is excluded, households with net worths of $1 million or more represent only 3.5 households per hundred of the US population. Stanley and Danko explain:

> America is still the land of opportunity. There is great pride, joy and satisfaction to be derived from building one's own fortune. Countless millionaires have told Stanley and Danko that the journey to wealth is much more satisfying than the destination. When they look back over their history of building wealth, they recall constantly setting economic goals and great happiness gained from achieving them. Yes, in the context of economic achievement it is the trip, the journey to financial independence about which the millionaire most often boasts.

It is fun to apply your creative juices to finding, buying, and making money from real estate.

The plan that is set down in the following chapters will provide a path to investment and realty wealth that is more likely to succeed than most other business opportunities. Each chapter is designed to enhance your understanding of the underlying fundamentals you'll need to

- find, negotiate, and buy income-producing property;
- structure your financing to ensure that you sign up for monthly payments that you can make (Within six months of purchase, mortgage payments should be no more than 45 percent of the building's scheduled gross income. If you adhere to this rule you automatically net 20 percent on rentals after expenses.);
- make only small down payments in order to limit your risk and increase the return on the cash you have available;

- make physical improvements to the property and improve the operations;
- refinance your property to fund your expansion when your equity reaches 50 percent; and
- take maximum advantage of depreciation benefits as allowed by the IRS.

With these fundamentals and a little experience looking for properties, you will learn to recognize properties whose value you can increase. In the chapter on financing you will learn creative ways to minimize your down payments and maximize the return on your available funds. You will become familiar with management techniques that you can apply immediately. The chapter on depreciation allowances shows ways to save money on taxes and turn it into spendable income. It is an up-to-date expansion—meant for today's market—of the principles that Bill Nickerson put forth in his classic real estate book, *How I Turned $1,000 into a Million in Real Estate—In My Spare Time*. These rules were also expanded upon by Albert J. Lowry in another quintessential book, *How You Can Become Financially Independent by Investing in Real Estate*.

Chapters 2 through 5 cover the fundamentals of investing in real estate. In chapter 6 you will learn to apply these fundamentals to building a property portfolio.

There are an estimated 10 million real estate investors in this country, and generally most have been successful and are independently wealthy. You can join this group too, but it's going to take hard work. Striking it rich in real estate is no tidy TV episode. Despite what the late night infomercial gurus tell you, you will need to learn the nuts and bolts of property management to create your foundation for success. You will also need to live below your means until you accomplish your goals. Saving for down payments and improvements will be an essential element of your success.

How long will this take? I'm sure there are many phenoms who obtained their lofty financial goals in as little as three or four years, but I've never met one. For most people, true success in real estate investment takes ten years or more—and we are talking about *true* investment income and cash flow, not phantom equity.

When you depend on properties to build wealth and a lifetime of income, you can achieve good returns, even in a recession. Values and rents can fall temporarily during down cycles; but when we return to a thriving economy, incomes and general prosperity push rents up. More households are formed as people can afford places of their own.

If you succeed at acquiring just five rental properties, you can build a lifetime of income and a generous monthly cash flow. I know because I did just that.

Michael E. Heeney
San Mateo, California

-1-

Create Investment Goals

If you believe in yourself and have dedication and pride—and never quit—you'll be a winner. The price of victory is high, but so are the rewards.

—Bear Bryant, football coach

Establish Your Investment Goals

You may ask, "What is the future of real estate?" Rest assured, your chances of making money in real estate are still very good. In recent history it is almost impossible to find any ten-year period in which real estate did not increase in value. Consider that the US population is predicted to increase nearly 30 percent during the period from 2000 to 2030, according to a 2005 report by the US Census Bureau (Figure 1). In Northern California, where I live, the population is predicted to increase almost 37 percent over the same time period. In most urban areas there is not an abundance of new rental housing under construction. Our population and income growth, in conjunction with the ongoing deterioration of existing buildings, will create plenty of opportunity for those who are interested.

There are dozens of ways to make money in real estate, including brokerage, trading, building, and fixing and selling (flipping), to name a few. Some ways are easier and more interesting than others, but the most remunerative way is to increase the value of buildings that you acquire by making them more attractive and up to date, thereby improving their potential for bringing in higher net rental income. Net rental income is what you put in your pocket after property expenses are paid. It is by far the fastest way to create wealth and independence. Your first objective should be to buy income property. Income property is, simply put, property in which you can generate income.

Implementing the fundamentals mentioned in the Introduction will offer you the most direct way to create a yearly income in investment real estate. Your goal could be to create a $200,000 annual income; this is the net profit, after expenses, on the properties you acquire. A net income in this range would establish your net worth to be in the range of $2 million—a 10 percent return on your investment.

Figure 1

Table 1: Interim Projections: Ranking of Census 2000 and Projected 2030 State Population and Change: 2000 to 2030

Census 2000 State	2000 Census Population	2000 Census Rank	2030 Projections State	2030 Projections Population	2030 Projections Rank	Change: 2000 to 2030 State	Change: 2000 to 2030 Number	Change: 2000 to 2030 Percent	Change: 2000 to 2030 Rank in percent change
United States	**281,421,906**	(x)	**United States**	**363,584,435**	(x)	**United States**	**82,162,529**	**29.2**	(x)
California	33,871,648	1	California	46,444,861	1	Nevada	2,283,845	114.3	1
Texas	20,851,820	2	Texas	33,317,744	2	Arizona	5,581,765	108.8	2
New York	18,976,457	3	Florida	28,685,769	3	Florida	12,703,391	79.5	3
Florida	15,982,378	4	New York	19,477,429	4	Texas	12,465,924	59.8	4
Illinois	12,419,293	5	Illinois	13,432,892	5	Utah	1,252,198	56.1	5
Pennsylvania	12,281,054	6	Pennsylvania	12,768,184	6	Idaho	675,671	52.2	6
Ohio	11,353,140	7	North Carolina	12,227,739	7	North Carolina	4,178,426	51.9	7
Michigan	9,938,444	8	Georgia	12,017,838	8	Georgia	3,831,385	46.8	8
New Jersey	8,414,350	9	Ohio	11,550,528	9	Washington	2,730,680	46.3	9
Georgia	8,186,453	10	Arizona	10,712,397	10	Oregon	1,412,519	41.3	10
North Carolina	8,049,313	11	Michigan	10,694,172	11	Virginia	2,746,504	38.8	11
Virginia	7,078,515	12	Virginia	9,825,019	12	Alaska	240,742	38.4	12
Massachusetts	6,349,097	13	New Jersey	9,802,440	13	California	12,573,213	37.1	13
Indiana	6,080,485	14	Washington	8,624,801	14	Colorado	1,491,096	34.7	14
Washington	5,894,121	15	Tennessee	7,380,634	15	New Hampshire	410,685	33.2	15
Tennessee	5,689,283	16	Maryland	7,022,251	16	Maryland	1,725,765	32.6	16

Census 2000 State	2000 Census Population	2000 Census Rank	2030 Projections State	2030 Projections Population	2030 Projections Rank	Change: 2000 to 2030 State	Change: 2000 to 2030 Number	Change: 2000 to 2030 Percent	Change: 2000 to 2030 Rank in percent change
Missouri	5,595,211	17	Massachusetts	7,012,009	17	Tennessee	1,691,351	29.7	17
Wisconsin	5,363,675	18	Indiana	6,810,108	18	Delaware	229,058	29.2	18
Maryland	5,296,486	19	Missouri	6,430,173	19	South Carolina	1,136,557	28.3	19
Arizona	5,130,632	20	Minnesota	6,306,130	20	Minnesota	1,386,651	28.2	20
Minnesota	4,919,479	21	Wisconsin	6,150,764	21	Arkansas	566,808	21.2	21
Louisiana	4,468,976	22	Colorado	5,792,357	22	Hawaii	254,509	21.0	22
Alabama	4,447,100	23	South Carolina	5,148,569	23	Vermont	103,040	16.9	23
Colorado	4,301,261	24	Alabama	4,874,243	24	New Jersey	1,388,090	16.5	24
Kentucky	4,041,769	25	Oregon	4,833,918	25	Montana	142,703	15.8	25
South Carolina	4,012,012	26	Louisiana	4,802,633	26	New Mexico	280,662	15.4	26
Oklahoma	3,450,654	27	Kentucky	4,554,998	27	Missouri	834,962	14.9	27
Oregon	3,421,399	28	Nevada	4,282,102	28	Wisconsin	787,089	14.7	28
Connecticut	3,405,565	29	Oklahoma	3,913,251	29	Oklahoma	462,597	13.4	29
Iowa	2,926,324	30	Connecticut	3,688,630	30	Kentucky	513,229	12.7	30
Mississippi	2,844,658	31	Utah	3,485,367	31	Indiana	729,623	12.0	31
Kansas	2,688,418	32	Arkansas	3,240,208	32	Maine	136,174	10.7	32
Arkansas	2,673,400	33	Mississippi	3,092,410	33	Massachusetts	662,912	10.4	33
Utah	2,233,169	34	Iowa	2,955,175	34	Rhode Island	104,622	10.0	34
Nevada	1,998,257	35	Kansas	2,940,084	35	Alabama	427,143	9.6	35
New Mexico	1,819,096	36	New Mexico	2,099,708	36	Kansas	251,666	9.4	36

Census 2000 State	2000 Census Population	2000 Census Rank	2030 Projections State	2030 Projections Population	2030 Projections Rank	Change: 2000 to 2030 State	Change: 2000 to 2030 Number	Change: 2000 to 2030 Percent	Change: 2000 to 2030 Rank in percent change
West Virginia	1,808,344	37	Idaho	1,969,624	37	Mississippi	247,752	8.7	37
Nebraska	1,711,263	38	Nebraska	1,820,247	38	Connecticut	283,065	8.3	38
Idaho	1,293,953	39	West Virginia	1,719,959	39	Illinois	1,013,599	8.2	39
Maine	1,274,923	40	New Hampshire	1,646,471	40	Michigan	755,728	7.6	40
New Hampshire	1,235,786	41	Hawaii	1,466,046	41	Louisiana	333,657	7.5	41
Hawaii	1,211,537	42	Maine	1,411,097	42	Nebraska	108,984	6.4	42
Rhode Island	1,048,319	43	Island	1,152,941	43	South Dakota	45,618	6.0	43
Montana	902,195	44	Montana	1,044,898	44	Wyoming	29,197	5.9	44
Delaware	783,600	45	Delaware	1,012,658	45	Pennsylvania	487,130	4.0	45
South Dakota	754,844	46	Alaska	867,674	46	New York	500,972	2.6	46
North Dakota	642,200	47	South Dakota	800,462	47	Ohio	197,388	1.7	47
Alaska	626,932	48	Vermont	711,867	48	Iowa	28,848	1.0	48
Vermont	608,827	49	North Dakota	606,566	49	West Virginia	-88,385	(4.9)	49
District of Columbia	572,059	50	Wyoming	522,979	50	North Dakota	-35,634	(5.5)	50
Wyoming	493,782	51	District of Columba	433,414	51	District of Columbia	-138,645	(24.2)	51

US Census Bureau, population Division, Interim State Population projections, 2005. Internet Release Date: April 21, 2005

Figure 1

Consider this important comparison: Suppose you bought and sold real estate and made $100,000 in one year, or earned $100,000 in some other business, or got a salary of $100,000. You would pay about $30,000 in taxes, leaving you with $70,000. If you invested it in a high-yielding bond, for example, with a return of 4 percent, you'd earn $2,400 a year. This is the long way to create a yearly income. It is difficult to earn a substantial sum beyond your salary. Even if you do, you can keep only part of it.

This book will show you a much easier and quicker way to create a worthwhile income. You will be surprised at the ease with which someone can build annuities in income-producing property.

Anyone with the confidence to take aim at the objective of financial independence has a good chance of success. Most experienced big-time owners expect a minimum operating net of 20 percent on their rents, after making their mortgage payments. The operating net is the net return from rental payments received while running the property; this is discussed further in the upcoming chapter on how to buy income property. In order to accomplish this objective, try to acquire property for which, within six months of purchase, the mortgage payments will equal no more than 45 percent of the scheduled gross income. In other words, after you improve the property and increase the rentals, your mortgage payments plus expenses (normally about 35 percent of the scheduled gross income) will leave you with 20 percent net (profit) of rents in your pocket.

In order to achieve a desired goal of $150,000 to $200,000 per year in operating net, you must have somewhere between $600,000 and $900,000 gross income from rentals. Since, for example, most buildings sell for six to nine times their gross income, you would need buildings valued at $5 million or more. In order to acquire buildings of that value, you would need approximately 25 percent down payment, or nearly $1.5 million, which is considered a normal transaction. The chapter on financing your acquisitions will show you how to minimize the down payment. A big bankroll is not necessary to get started; however, you will need lots of persistence.

Most of the concepts included in later chapters are simple to grasp, although they are not always easy to implement. You will need to overcome many obstacles, up to and including your own emotions. It has been said that the *character* of the would-be millionaire is more important than that person's type of business. There is no doubt that it takes a little imagination, persistence, and enterprise to accomplish your stated objectives of financial independence.

However, real estate lends itself to leverage like no other business. Leverage is using mostly other people's money to finance your properties. Most lenders will lend up to 70 percent loan to value (LTV) on your income property. As much as money wholesalers like banks need savers to provide them with funds, they also depend on investors to borrow that money. You and I can use this for highly profitable enterprises.

As an example, I once met a family of four brothers who operated a handsome twelve-story high-rise office building in a nearby city. They had built the property in the mid-1960s for a cost of about $4 million (most of which was borrowed). Today their heirs benefit from the substantial income that the building produces. The value of the building now is about $35 million.

Consider real estate operator Joseph Kennedy's 1945 purchase of the Merchandise Mart in Chicago. At that time, the Merchandise Mart was the world's largest commercial building. Kennedy bought the Merchandise Mart for approximately $13 million. He was able to obtain a $12.5 million insurance company loan, which made his down payment only $500,000, or less than 4 percent.

Marshall Field, the Chicago retailer and original owner of the Merchandise Mart, sold to Kennedy at a sacrifice because his firm, strong in merchandizing, was rather rigid as an income property operator. Field was afraid of heavy vacancies that might come from the impending loss of government tenants, who occupied about a third of the building at low rents. To an imaginative income property investor like Kennedy, this presented an opportunity. Under his management, the Merchandise Mart leased to commercial tenants at considerably higher rents.

Four years after Kennedy's purchase, the increase in value enabled him to get a new $17 million insurance company loan. This gave him $4 million over his purchase price to use for some property improvements and for further investment. In 1998, the Kennedy heirs sold the Merchandise Mart (the only building with its own postal zip code) for approximately $369 million.

You can emulate big-time realty investors, as in the examples above, by adhering to certain key objectives:

- Buying property with a proven history of rising rents
- Putting up as small a down payment as possible and arranging for monthly payments that you know you can make
- Improving the property in ways that will increase its rental value
- Refinancing the property to fund your expansion when your equity grows to 50 percent or more

If you use the methods described in this book you can obtain an initial goal of $1 million net worth in as little as ten years. Your progress will depend on the economic cycle during the time you choose to implement your plan. Since competition makes it difficult to acquire property during good economic times, the methods outlined here work better during slow or recessionary times. For example, during the real estate bubble years of 2001 to 2006, making sensible acquisitions was difficult because of the tremendous demand for just about any kind of real estate. So, as you can see, your progress could be slowed at times when demand for real estate is high. During contracting economic times, you can expect acquisitions to speed up.

When you invest in real estate, you can see and control what your dollars are doing. Very little luck is involved in your profit and loss. Nearly all the factors can be examined ahead of time, so your own efforts and common sense count heavily.

You make money by going into debt when you invest in real estate. Common strategies for profits include

- staying as deeply in debt as possible with safety (As Walt Disney once said, "I must be rich, I owe five million dollars.");
- making maximum use of depreciation allowances and other tax saving methods (Depreciation benefits can shelter a good percentage of your operating net income.); and
- improving your property and refinancing it as soon as you can.

Even if you are not looking to be a millionaire, real estate may still provide very positive benefits. For instance, you may create a side income that will supplement your salary or wages. You could progress to one small apartment house and concentrate on paying down the mortgage and getting the property free and clear of debt. Real estate can serve as a part-time job. This business is easier than most to keep within whatever limits of time and capital you have available. You can put all of your capital into it and work full-time, or you can invest just a little money or time. You'll have to study real estate enough to know whether or not brokers and managers are offering you good advice. The novices who do well in real estate are those who put some time into it.

Most find it an alluring endeavor as well as a road to financial security.

Chapter Recap

Due to population increases, demand for real estate should expand in the future.

- Concentrate on properties in which you can easily generate income.
- Continue to build up your rental income by making acquisitions year after year until you accomplish your financial goals.

-2-

Selecting Your Investment Property

On Confidence: Self-assurance is two-thirds of success.

—Unknown

What Type of Property Should You Buy?

The first step in all of this is to determine what type of property you should buy. Should you buy commercial property or residential apartments? Commercial property could be classified as retail, industrial, or office property. Residential dwellings would include duplex housing, fourplexes, and small to large multiunit apartment buildings.

Some of the advantages of commercial property include limited management responsibilities. There are not as many "people problems" as there can be with residential dwelling structures. The big difference is that there are people *living* in residential structures 24/7. And as the owner, you are responsible for the property at all times. If the air conditioning goes out in the middle of a hot summer, you are the one that the tenants call. A residential owner must stay on top of the property's upkeep because you have entered into a contract with your tenant to do so. You need to know that most municipalities require residential owners to comply with a lengthy list of habitability issues.

This is not true with most commercial properties. Most commercial tenants are tied to long-term leases, which can be another benefit to the landlord. Many commercial businesses, if they are successful, want to stay in their locations for many years. This makes for much less tenant turnover for the owner. Some leases are written so that the tenant is responsible for property taxes, insurance, utilities, and maintenance. In other words, the tenant—not the landlord—has to carry the burden for the ever-increasing operating costs.

Some of the disadvantages of commercial property include long-term leases that limit your ability to increase rental income. Residential dwellings have more frequent turnover, allowing the owner the opportunity to make selected improvements while increasing the rental income. Apartments, therefore, lend themselves more readily to selling for capital gains. Also consider that land costs cannot be depreciated. Depreciation is a method by which the IRS allows you to recover a portion of the cost of your building during your ownership. However, the land cost of your purchase price is excluded. The fact that land costs cannot be depreciated is a drawback to commercial property ownership. Commercial property land costs are proportionately high compared with most building values. With apartment buildings, where land values are usually much less, a much higher proportion of total costs can be charged off as depreciation. This goes a long way in reducing taxes owed on your operating income.

Commercial property can be very slow to sell and just as slow to lease, with vacancies sometimes lasting for very extended periods of time. You would need a large surplus of income to sustain the property during these periods.

Due to these disadvantages, a beginner should probably avoid commercial property. Entering the commercial real estate market on a large scale would require a very high tax bracket and a large surplus of income, plus experience and know-how that most investors do not have. Your best opportunities will be with dwelling units, from fourplexes to small to midsize apartment buildings.

Should you buy unimproved land? Unimproved land is real estate that hasn't been properly set up with electricity, water service, street access, or phone service. It is, as advertised, a chunk of land. I recommend avoiding unimproved land, especially if you are a beginner, and always if you are working with limited capital. There are good opportunities in land, and a lot of fortunes have been made there; but these fortunes were made by individuals who could afford to buy on speculation. You can only let the land sit with the hope that it will become more valuable later down the road.

During the waiting period, landowners are willing to make substantial mortgage and real estate tax payments out of their pockets, with little or no income from the land. Also, like commercial property, land is slow to sell, and when it does sell the seller usually has to carry the financing for a large percentage of the purchase price. This can tie up your funds for years. During the waiting period before a substantial value increase, you could have pyramided that same initial investment into a large income by investing in rent-producing property. So you can see where the problems lie with investing in unimproved land.

Given that, it is generally a good idea to start with apartments. This book will show you how to evaluate, finance, and improve apartments. They are in demand in every part of the country. As a general rule you should buy the greatest number of units available for the money you can afford to invest. And you should make the smallest down payment possible. Your percentage yield will be bigger with a smaller down payment, provided your mortgage payments are not too high.

The more units there are in your property, the better off you'll be. This is because the overhead and many of the fixed expenses are proportionately lower when spread over more units. However, if you are just beginning, you should probably start with a fourplex and expand as you gain experience.

And do not be seduced by the prestige of owning a beautiful building. You will recognize these when they are advertised as offering "pride of ownership." Usually the most profitable investments are fourplexes and apartments buildings that can be improved and are located in moderate-income neighborhoods.

As of this writing, seizing upon the growing demand and the dearth of new construction, apartment landlords nationwide have boosted rents over the last two years and expect to keep raising them for the foreseeable future.

The improving fundamentals have placed multifamily properties well ahead in occupancy and rent growth as compared to other commercial real estate sectors, which in many cases are experiencing anemic growth.

With the renter-age population plentiful and with many financially strapped homeowners turning into tenants, monthly apartment rents are on the rise. These factors suggest that we will see unusual growth in the apartment sector over the next few years.

Selecting a Good Location

The best area in which to locate properties with good potential for improving—which is what this book is all about—is a somewhat older area with many different styles and types of structures. Such areas usually contain many neglected buildings or buildings in need of remodeling. The older areas also offer more opportunity to use your skill at finding properties that are priced below market value.

To contrast, finding an underpriced property in a fairly new area is relatively difficult. First the seller probably has not owned the property very long; thus you must contend with the price he paid for it. Secondly, it can take quite a number of years for a property to become outdated or deteriorated enough to provide a substantial rehabilitation opportunity. Older neighborhoods offer more opportunities for the kind of property you are looking for to create the possibility of large capital gains.

Keep in mind that you will almost certainly make a mistake if you buy one of the first properties you see without looking at many others. You need the experience gained by comparing the good and bad points of many different properties. You will begin to develop this skill as you look at more real estate.

You should also concentrate on average income rentals and tenants rather than luxury apartments. High-end luxury rentals are usually hit with vacancies during economic recessions because of the small percentage of prospective tenants.

The number-one rule in locating a good property is that the property should offer maximum possibilities to increase value. The building's structure should be sound so that you can make improvements that will bring the building up to date at a lower total cost than what new construction would require.

At the time of purchase, the property should pay a decent return in order to pay for the mortgage payments and operating expenses. Your goal should be to obtain a net 20 percent return on rentals within six months of purchase; you can expect to reach this goal after you complete necessary improvements. Each mortgage principal payment that is derived from the property itself increases your net worth to the extent that it reduces the outstanding loan balance. It is like that old saying, "This thing pays for itself." It is a forced savings plan.

To get started, drive around several neighborhoods, eliminating some and spending more time in others as you get a feel for them. You can use the checklist below to determine the good and not-so-desirable characteristics of neighborhoods. Try to find a neighborhood in the path of the city's growth—a portion of the city that is attracting higher-income residents, or is being gentrified or is beginning to be developed by builders. Rents have a tendency to rise under these circumstances. You want low-priced property that you can upgrade quickly. You probably won't find bargains in luxurious high-rent districts. In cities all across America, downtowns are being redeveloped to accommodate a desire to be closer to jobs and cultural activities. These changes present tremendous opportunities to build a solid realty fortune.

You will need to examine as many properties as possible. As we've already discussed, you should look for fourplexes and small apartment buildings. You will need to become a detective. There will be a ton of information to uncover, such as current neighborhood rents, asking prices per unit, and you should look at past and present lease terms to determine the rate of turnover in the area. Talk to the local mailman when you see him or her. You will be surprised what they can tell you about the neighborhood vacancy rate.

Neighborhood Checklist

Use this checklist when you are investigating neighborhoods.

- **Safety.** Is the area well lit at night? Are there people hanging out?
- **Development.** Is there any new construction in the area? New construction often brings a rise in property values.

- **Noise and Congestion.** Is there congestion? At what time of day? Are there factories or noisy freeways close by? Appraisers often deduct value for these and other factors that may reduce expected rent.

- **Employment Centers.** Does the location offer easy access to the area's employment centers? Is there public transportation to take tenants there?

- **Crime.** Many cities offer crime reports online for individual neighborhoods. The local police department is an excellent source for specific information concerning crime in neighborhoods or on streets you may be interested in.

- **Quality of Schools.** This is important for families that you may rent to. How close are the schools, and what reputation do they have? Are the schools within walking distance, or is public or other transportation required to reach them?

- **Marginal Districts.** Do some buildings look dilapidated and vulnerable to fire? Are there boarded-up buildings in the area? If so, you'd better find another neighborhood. It can be difficult to even get insurance in these types of areas.

- **Distance from Your Home.** You should consider the distance from your home to any neighborhood in which you invest. You should be at most a one-hour drive from your investment. I suggest you manage your own investments when you start out, not only to save money but also to gain experience.

- **Range of Rents.** An area where monthly rents range between $500 and $1,200 might contain good buys. The range of rents in a given neighborhood will be one of the most important pieces of information you'll need. Ideally, you want a building where rents are somewhat below average. This is so you won't price yourself out of the market when you improve it and raise the rent. You can find information about rents by talking to apartment managers in the area.

Once you have an idea of prevailing rents in an area, you can estimate building value. Most apartment buildings sell for between six and nine times their gross income. Information on most of the above items on the checklist can be gleaned from talking to area apartment managers. Pick a manager whose building has few vacancies, as indicated by names on mailboxes.

I have found that area apartment managers provide more reliable information about various districts than, say, real estate agents. When there is a substantial commission on the line, an agent's self-interest can make him less objective; it's human nature.

Once you are familiar with several promising districts, you are then ready for the next step, which is to dig deeper. Remember, you are in detective mode now.

Take note of any buildings that have peeling paint or overgrown weeds in the front or that offer any other hints that the property is rundown. Make a note of these addresses even if the buildings are not for sale. A mismanaged property in a fairly decent location is the kind of opportunity you are seeking. The neglect is a clue that the owner may not be even thinking about the property. If you suggest it to him, he may jump at the chance to sell. You can get the owner's name and address from your local tax assessor's records, which are made available to the public. From there you may either phone the owner or write a letter. If you are uncomfortable doing that, ask a real estate agent to do it for you. Also, try working with agents who have property listings in the areas that interest you.

Most mismanaged properties are owned by people who are no longer interested in owning them and are even less interested in managing them. Often the owner of a mismanaged property turns out to be the widow or heir of the original owner, or the property might be owned by a partnership that is not working out. Sometimes the owner is an absentee landlord trying unsuccessfully to manage the property from a distance. Sometimes he or she is ill—or is in financial difficulty, unable to pay for repairs and maintenance because the rent money is needed for other purposes.

In any of these situations, the owner probably isn't making much money from the property. His tenants surely aren't paying top rents, and they are more than likely causing all kinds of trouble for the owner. For all these reasons, the owner of this sort of property may be receptive to your offer to buy, and you will be on your way to big profits!

Chapter Recap

In this chapter we learned that most investors should start with apartments.

- Older properties located in established neighborhoods are more likely to yield good buys.
- You should concentrate on average income rentals rather than luxury apartments.
- Look for buildings that are structurally sound so you can make improvements that will bring the building up to date for less than the cost of new construction.
- Drive around several neighborhoods that interest you. Talk to apartment managers to determine prevailing rents in the area. Contact brokers that have listings in these areas.

-3-

How to Negotiate a Good Deal

If you want to achieve a high goal, you're going to have to take some chances.

—*Alberto Salazar, marathon runner and coach*

In making offers and negotiating prices with sellers and real estate brokers, you should be aware of the factors that can affect the value and profitability of operating an apartment building. Ask yourself these questions:

- What kinds of tenants are in the building?
- What kinds of apartments are in the building?
- What improvements will be profitable?
- What expenses can I expect?
- What can I do to make the property more attractive?
- What is the value of the building?
- What type of seller should I buy from?
- Are the variables negotiable?

Existing Tenants Can Be Crucial to Your Investment
The existing tenants of an apartment building can be crucial to your investment decision. Do not be afraid to talk to them to get an idea of what you can expect, based on what they expect. The fair price of an

apartment building depends on the income from rents. But be careful, some sellers make concessions to their tenants. Such concessions can be as follows:

- The owner could be permitting the tenant to pay less than the full rent stated on the rental agreement.
- The owner could be paying the tenant's utility bills even though the building may be separately metered.
- The owner could be offering substantial discounts on the stated rent for tenants who pay on time.
- The owner could be providing groceries for some tenants.
- The owner may permit some tenants to intermittently skip paying rent in some months.
- The owner may allow some tenants rental discounts for keeping the property clean.

Concessions are sometimes unavoidable in a soft rental market, but they are also a way for an unscrupulous seller to inflate the rental income. Do not be misled into thinking you are acquiring a building full of tenants who are paying the full rental rates twelve months a year if they are not. If concessions have been made or if tenants are behind on rent, you should lower your purchase offer accordingly.

Always make your purchase offer contingent on approval of inspections, such as the following:

- Seeing the interior of each unit
- Approving the inspections the owner has had done on the building (including termite and any environmental reports)
- Inspecting the books to verify the actual income collected and expenses paid (Check rental agreements and receipts given for rents. In some cases, the utility companies can advise you of past usage for the subject property. Property taxes can be projected based on your purchase price.)

Keep in mind that, until you have actually tendered an offer to buy, you probably will not be able to inspect any apartments except the vacant ones. But you can make an offer "subject to inspection of the interior." With your offer in hand, the owner will be willing to show the apartments. Insist on seeing them all. If the seller says he "doesn't have keys for" one or two apartments or if he makes other suspect excuses, insist on seeing those units, even if you need to return another day.

What Kind of Tenants Are Most Profitable?

Most owners would prefer two adults—with no pets or children—who are employed and away from home most of the time. You are probably on track to make a high-profit investment if you find a building occupied mostly by couples or elderly folks who have lived there for years. They are rooted to their apartments, and they will probably stay unless you boost the rent out of sight.

Never allow an occupant with a large dog to reside in your building. This is especially true in apartment buildings. Considering the dense nature of an apartment building, the risk is too great.

Whether a building accepts children and pets may indicate the rentability and profit margin of the units. If units stay vacant, owners start accepting children and pets. The pressures of competition can force concessions, and renting to less desirable tenants is one of those concessions. The more concessions a building is making, the higher its expenses. Expenses such as utilities can be substantially higher under these circumstances. This would increase along with the number of people living in the unit.

Even with good management you must expect some turnover. Forecast your maintenance budget accordingly. Tenant ages, occupations, and workplaces, as shown on the rental applications, are worth thinking about when comparing and negotiating for properties.

Mixture of Units in Building

The types of buildings can tell you much about what to expect from occupants, and what sort of changes will or will not pay off.

If a building has a mixture of three-bedroom units and studio apartments, you would have a hard time managing it. Your tenants would be different types with different needs. Ill-assorted tenants make a building hard to manage and hard to rent. The unit mix, as it is called, is a factor in profitability.

In another example, if you have a building with all studio apartments, you can expect above-average turnover. Maintenance and vacancy costs tend to be high in these types of buildings due to the transitional nature of the tenants. These units are sometimes referred to as "efficiency apartments."

Some banks are reluctant to make new first trust deed loans, or mortgages, on all-studio buildings. Without exceptional management, the vacancy factor can be quite high due to the frequent turnover.

Suppose a building has only three-bedroom units. Can it be a good investment? Maybe. Its residents would be families with children, so you would need to know how close the schools are and how good the schools are. You would also need to take into account your probable costs for frequent cleaning, painting, and repairs. Children run up the bills. So the question is whether your prospective occupants could, and would, pay the unusually high rents you would have to charge.

In some smaller properties that you examine (say, five units and less), be aware of illegal units or conversions. An illegal unit could be a living space or apartment created without city approval or permission. Sometimes owners convert basement space into apartments. Often the ceiling heights in these units do not conform to local building codes, and frequently these illegal units and conversions have tiny kitchens with small refrigerators and hot plates instead of stoves.

Natural conversions of property are made when the space converted may be used as a standard dwelling unit and looks as though it might have been included in the original building design. Examples, which may attract tenants, are attics and aboveground basements, full-sized for square footage and height. Unnatural conversions are made by using space that is unsuitable or too limited, or by creating awkward subdivisions of standard units. These ugly types of conversions suffer high vacancy and turnover factors.

Similar to lenders' reluctance to make loans on all-studio unit buildings, many appraisers and lenders will not count the projected income from awkward conversions and illegal units. And there are many of them, particularly within older properties located in inner-city areas.

Buildings that have a mixture of one- and two-bedroom apartments can represent your best opportunities.

What Type of Improvements Are Profitable?

In sizing up an income property, you should know exactly what improvements you will have to make, as well as approximately what they will cost, before deciding whether to buy the property. You should make them only if they will heighten the property's attractiveness to tenants—because this should mean higher rents, which in turn mean higher value.

Improvements that would be profitable in one property might be wasted in another. They must appeal to the type of people who are likely to rent in the neighborhood. So here again, you need to know about your occupants. Always keep potential occupants in mind while you are looking at income property and considering possible improvements.

You might wonder why you should make property improvements at all. If you do not keep up a property, its market value will keep sinking because the next buyer—assuming you can find one—will subtract the cost of making those deferred improvements from the amount he is willing to pay.

You will never have a chance to make a property more profitable than when you can count on the property being filled. This is when your property is operating at its maximum. It is good business to invest some of the net income in improvements; this helps ensure that your building will continue to operate to its highest potential. Besides, there are always people who will pay a better price for a better product. If the present renters cannot afford the higher rents, there will be others who can, so long as you do not charge more than the existing top rents in the area.

When you are deciding on a real estate investment, choose one you can improve. Once you are sure what its maximum potential rents will be, then do your homework to see how much upgrading or remodeling will be necessary.

General Expenses for Apartment Buildings/Net Income

In figuring your net income from the property, you will want to allow for vacancies, bad debts, utility expenses, taxes, insurance, and repair costs. How much should you allow for these expenses? A summary of general expenses for apartment buildings is below.

- **Insurance.** Quotes for insurance can be very competitive in most markets. Be sure to get adequate liability insurance.
- **Property Taxes.** Check with local brokers as to what your new real estate taxes will be. For example, in California, under Proposition 13, taxes are about 1.2 percent of the purchase price, plus any voter-approved supplemental taxes. In some cities there are also license fees, which must be paid annually.
- **Utilities.** This would include bills for local pickup of trash at your buildings as well as local charges for gas and electricity. In many cases, buildings have one hot water heater for all tenants, and the landlord pays for the gas to operate it. It is a huge advantage to you if you can find buildings where tenants have their own water heaters for which they pay for their own hot water expense. You also need to be cognizant of charges for water at your properties; in almost all cases you will be paying one bill for water usage at your building. It is very rare to find a building that is separately metered for water, thereby enabling the tenants to pay for their own usage. I have found some buildings built in the 1940s that are separately metered for water, but this type of building is extremely uncommon.
- **Maintenance.** The national average for maintenance on apartment buildings is approximately 8 percent of gross income for the property. This expense includes everything you need to spend to keep the property up and rented but does not include capital expenses and improvements. Maintenance can include repainting

and recarpeting a vacancy, for example. Eight percent of gross income is simply a ballpark figure. It can vary from building to building, depending on age and whether you do your own work or hire a contractor. It can also vary between owners of the same property. You should calculate projected expenses for maintenance on a building-by-building basis. Try not to use the seller's computation of expenses because, more than likely, your style of management will be different. This is especially true if you are taking over for an owner whose operating practices were less than desirable. Factor in a nominal sum for a resident manager who may be doing some maintenance.

- **Vacancy Factor.** The national average is about 5 percent of gross income on the building, though this can vary depending on the local economy. With good management, you can reduce this factor down to 3 percent or less. However, if you are employing a management company, normally this expense will be somewhat higher.

The sum of the above expenses can average about 35 percent of the scheduled income that the building produces. The balance left over after deducting these expenses is referred to as your net income. You pay your mortgage payment from the net income, and any balance that remains after the mortgage is paid would be considered profit. A portion of that should be kept in reserves for replacements such as a new roof, exterior painting, or other capital expenses.

What Can I Do to Make It More Attractive?

Look at the entryway to the property. Are there ways you can make it more attractive? Look at the front steps, lobby, and hallways. Maybe fresh paint and new carpeting or tile would increase attractiveness.

First impressions can be crucial. Prospective residents must be impressed when they walk in the front entrance. If not, they will walk out again, unless there is an extreme shortage of apartments. So you should plan to make enough improvements in the entrance, lobby, and halls to give you a clean, competitive edge over other buildings in the neighborhood.

If your building has children, barren backyards can be converted to play areas with picnic tables and barbecues. Attractive landscaping can boost occupancy.

New exterior paint can be the best investment you can make. Many income properties built in the 1960s are now being upgraded with new double pane windows. This not only saves on tenant energy bills but also adds to the attractiveness of the building. Unfortunately, most owners do very little to make improvements to their buildings

An expert should check the heating, wiring, plumbing, roofs, and foundation of the building. Sometimes rewiring the electrical system can be worthwhile. Often this significantly reduces your electrical and insurance costs. You do not normally get increased rent from replacing the roof or the foundation, but these improvements can be a selling point to potential tenants.

If you discover a leaky roof that leaks in only one place, you can normally patch it. Leaks in multiple places warrant a complete roof replacement. I have replaced the roofs on every property I have acquired. In any building you are contemplating acquiring, if the roof is more than fifteen years old, you will probably need to replace it.

You should work up a list of the property's faults, curable and incurable. You want the former, as most of them are valuable. You do not want the latter, as they cut down your possible profit and may rule out the property altogether as a profitable investment. Valuable faults are those that you will profit from correcting because you can get higher rents after correcting such deficiencies.

Two such valuable deficiencies are worn-out landscaping and exterior paint. Others are walls that badly need paint or plaster, worn carpets, shabby blinds or drapes, antiquated light and plumbing fixtures (especially in kitchens or bathrooms), inadequate heating, or incompetent managers.

In other words, a curable deficiency is almost anything that can be fixed up at a reasonable cost and will make an apartment worth a higher rent to the kind of person who lives in that area. These flaws are the signs of a potentially good investment.

You cannot do much about a bad floor plan, bad neighborhood, lack of parking, narrow halls, small rooms, cramped closet space, or sloping walls or floors. That is why these incurable defects shrink your potential profits.

You can repair a rotten foundation, but this will not make the building more inviting to current tenants, so it is not a valuable defect. The same is true of a leaky roof. Fixing the roof will not justify raising the rents.

In short, whatever emergency repairs are needed must be classed as undesirable defects, and you must deduct the cost from the price you are willing to offer for the property. Deferred maintenance reduces the value of the property.

What Is the Value of the Building?

Bankers and appraisers of income property use three approaches to determine values:

- Comparison approach
- Replacement cost approach
- Income approach

The *comparison approach* is used most often with properties containing one to four units, including single-family homes. This method simply compares similar properties in the same neighborhood to the subject property for which you are determining value. Factors such as the number of rooms, square footage, and various amenities lend themselves to comparison. Comparable sales of similar properties in the neighborhood can be analyzed. The more similar the properties are, the more easily you can compare them. So do not try to compare single-family homes with duplexes, or a garden-court apartment home with a ten-story high rise. Unless you confine your comparisons to neighborhoods that appear to be about equal, you may be badly fooled. If you are not sure whether properties you want to compare are really in the same neighborhood, go talk to a few local real estate people.

Square footage is probably the most important point of comparison. People prefer spacious rooms and closets. So if one building has more usable space than another, tenants may be willing to pay higher rents there. If you know the current rentals, you can compile the amount of income per square foot—a useful yardstick in comparing properties. Making these close comparisons will give you valuable experience. Each time you do it, your analysis will be faster and easier.

The *replacement cost approach* is another method of figuring the approximate value of property. You arrive at this by taking into account the value of the land, the age of the building, and the cost of reconstructing it. Since costs were doubtless much lower when it was built, you go by today's costs rather than those of years ago. In order to figure the cost per square foot to build, consult a local contractor's association, or mortgage lenders. Once you have the number to reconstruct the property, you need to depreciate approximately 40 percent of the building if it is twenty years old. Depreciate the building about 2 percent per year, but do not include the land. Finally, you add the land value to these figures. Brokers and bankers can usually tell you the value of land anywhere in town.

The *income approach* to value may be the most useful because, as a realty investor you are buying a stream of income. The actual income is what the units are now producing in rents. The scheduled income is what the broker or seller says the total income should be when all units are rented. Most apartment buildings sell for between six and nine times their scheduled income. Variations depend on the neighborhood, age, and condition of the property you are considering.

Say you find a twelve-unit building with identical apartments. You might find that ten are actually rented for $850 a month—but the two that are vacant are scheduled on the books at $950 a month. You are unlikely to get that much until you upgrade them, since they are the same as those that are now renting for $850. Thus, you need to use your own income projections and not the seller's or his broker's projections.

As previously discussed, your objective is to determine the true income that the building produces. Deduct the following costs from the sum of the rents that are truly coming in each month:

- Allowances for vacancies (about 5 percent of scheduled income)

- Monthly utilities expenses, including water, gas, electricity, and garbage services
- Maintenance (normally about 8 percent of scheduled income per property)
- Property taxes, licenses, and insurance

After deducting these items, make allowance for the mortgage payments. You should have money left over each month.

Your true monthly net income is an important consideration. If it will be small and will barely cover your mortgage payments, then you should probably pass on the investment. Do not tie up your capital in a piece of real estate that will generate low net income, if there is any chance you may need that capital somewhere else.

When you get down to serious consideration of a possible buy, you need to find out the true total of rent collected during the past several years. You also need to determine the true expenses. You can verify these expenses through utility companies, public records for taxes, and the maintenance, which can be estimated.

Once you know the true net income, it may point you to a good buy. When net is abnormally low, you can harp on this in negotiating with the owner and the broker. Try to press them to lower the asking price. This is where playing the detective really pays off.

Determining the *capitalization rate* is an important part of the income approach to evaluating your proposed investment. The capitalization rate is arrived at by dividing the annual net income by the estimate of value. It is commonly used by brokers and bankers in determining the "value" of income properties. You can find this if you know the selling prices for various properties in the vicinity, and if you know their annual net incomes. To get the capitalization rate on that transaction, divide the annual net income by the price (which was the market's estimate of value). If you know the net income that a building produces, and if you know the rate of return or yield for the neighborhood, you can determine the market value by dividing the net income by the rate of yield (or capitalization rate, as it is called) to get the building's market value. Below is a chart to help visualize this concept.

Property	Annual Net	Sales Price	Capitalization Rate
A	$76,933	$1,100,000	0.0699/7%
B	$165,960	$2,370,857	0.0700/7%
C	$18,900	$186,556	0.1013/10%
D	$91,634	$1,500,000	0.0610/6%

Basically, the higher the capitalization rate, the lower the price. Using only a few transactions to compute the going rate may allow distorting factors in some of the deals to have an impact—things such as forced sales, errors in computation, and any number of other possibilities. But if you collect enough data on a large number of transactions, the distorting factors will offset each other, and you will see the pattern.

Since you are probably not going to take all that trouble, you may be willing to take the word of real estate experts, who make such surveys all the time. They say that the capitalization rate varies greatly from one neighborhood to another, but it averages about 7.5 percent in my area.

To recap, you should never pay more than the income value or the replacement value—whichever is less. If you hold to the principal of buying older property on the basis of existing income, you will always buy for less than the cost of replacement. Your capitalized price will often be considerably less than the replacement cost. This enables you to maintain an enviable competitive position with low initial cost:

- You can rent below the market for comparable new housing.
- You can successfully compete with new housing, in terms of appearance, with selective renovations.
- You can successfully compete with older housing, which fails to match your renovation.

What Type of Seller Should You Buy From?

A good businessperson does not try to take advantage of the other party in a buying/selling transaction. It is bad business in the long run, because word gets around and people do not want to deal with anyone with a poor reputation. This is especially true if you plan to acquire multiple income properties over a long period of time in the same city. On multiple occasions, large income property owners have sold additional parcels of their mismanaged property to me because I have been fair in my dealings with them. So it is smart to strike a bargain that is fair to both sides.

It is also important not to set your heart on a specific building as the one and only buy for you. Many amateur buyers fall into this trap; emotions override common sense, causing them to pay too much. If any owner senses you are set on buying, he will stand firm on his asking price—and it will usually be too high.

Some owners never come down from sky-high prices, despite all logic. You need to be emotionally prepared to walk away without disappointment. You should always be looking for other potential buys that you have not looked at before. Mismanaged property—the kind you have been looking for—exists almost everywhere. Much of it is never advertised or publicly listed.

More than likely, you are the only prospective buyer for whatever rundown buildings you ask about. Real estate is worth whatever people will pay. It is up to you to negotiate a price. When you are buying depressed real estate, never forget that you are in a strong bargaining position because there is very little demand for what you want to buy.

I make it a habit to go to the county tax assessor's office or website and get a copy of the tax bill for any property that I am considering. From this bill you can determine how much the taxes are, as well as when the seller originally purchased the property and for what price. You can also get the owner's name and address.

In most transactions, using an intermediary is a smart choice. Rely on your broker. They have more experience than you do in putting deals together. Face-to-face bargaining rarely works well in real estate. Pride of ownership may get in the way. Personalities may clash. But middlemen with expertise in realty negotiations can keep the emotion out of the bickering and figure out solutions that might never occur to the principals.

Usually you can make a better deal with someone who has owned a property for ten years or more. He probably bought it when prices were lower, and his tax benefits from depreciation could now be much smaller. He probably has a lot of equity, which opens up the chance for you to refinance the building and come in with a smaller down payment. Equity is the difference between the mortgage and the market value of the property, and the size of the owner's equity is an important guide to your negotiation tactics.

A small equity in the property is usually a tipoff to a recent purchase, but it could also mean that the owner refinanced the building and pulled out cash within the last year or so. Either way, when an owner with little equity seems eager to sell, and willing to compromise on price, he is probably in a personal predicament that makes him desperate. He may haggle stubbornly because he needs every dollar he can squeeze out of the deal.

I have found it far easier to negotiate with an owner who has a large equity. Options for financing are much greater, as we will see in the next chapter.

Buyers and sellers who dislike bargaining may establish a firm figure and say, "That's my price. Take it or leave it." People who do this in real estate transactions are usually left with poorer deals than they could have realized through negotiation—or without any deal at all. After a certain amount of back and forth, the average seller, especially if his place has been on the market for several months, will accept an offer as much as 25 percent under his original asking price, although he would have refused that low a number as an initial offer. A competent realtor often convinces this seller to set a price near market value, so the broker's listing may already be considerably lower than the seller's initial asking price. Subtracting 10 to 25 percent from the asking price is, of course, no final gauge of value, since the knowing seller will price high to begin with.

Before making an offer, you should establish both the lowest price the seller might accept and then the top price you will pay. That way you are not likely to be swayed by subsequent sales pressure.

Negotiable Variables

Typically in any real estate deal, four variables must be negotiated:

- Purchase price
- Down payment
- Interest rate on any loan involved
- Length of time in which to repay loan

These variables are very common in negotiating to buy investment property. Some buyers hate to pay interest and prefer large equities. But using borrowed money to purchase income property is one of the secrets of financial success. The more leverage you can use, the bigger your profit will be.

Sometimes in negotiating these four variables, it might be good business to accept a higher purchase price (or a price closer to what the seller is asking) in exchange for a lower down payment. Conversely if you intend to make a large down payment, you should seek a substantial discount off the asking price. Normally any loan carried for you on the property by the seller is considered seller financing. You may ask the seller to do this for you in the event that you cannot make a large enough down payment to qualify for a new conventional first mortgage—or if you find that interest rates on new mortgages from conventional sources are simply too high. You might also consider this option if you anticipate that the property you are negotiating to buy will not qualify for a new mortgage due to its present condition.

The buyer can take the existing loan on the property "subject to" (discussed in chapter 4) or formally assume the loan, and the seller can carry a loan on the property that would represent the difference between the buyer's down payment and the sum of the existing loans. This is more fully explained in chapter 4, "Financing Your Acquisitions."

An owner may give you favorable terms on some of these variables in exchange for concessions from you on other variables. This give and take is part of the bargaining process. It is why sellers ask a higher price than they hope to get, and why buyers offer less than they are willing to pay.

Keep in mind that in realty transactions buyers and sellers make their largest concessions early in the game. The seller will drop the price more in the first round of negotiations than he will later. As bargaining progresses, the seller usually sticks to his position longer and longer.

Whenever possible, be prepared to yield something in early negotiations but do not indicate that you will grant further concessions. Phrase each offer as though it is a final offer, yet be sure to word it loosely enough that you can change it without losing face.

The buyer's objective is to learn all the seller's problems, goals, and inclinations. For example, let's say you find out that you are negotiating with an elderly seller who does not want to maintain the property any longer; this will impact how you move forward. Conversely, from the buyer's standpoint, the less the seller knows about the buyer, the better.

A final point on this: the buyer should show no enthusiasm or great interest in the property he is offering to buy.

Many property buyers use online listings and newspaper classified ads to become acquainted with various brokers and to look for ads in their price range and location. Look to online sources such as Loopnet (www.loopnet. com) for the largest Web site listing service for commercial properties, especially apartment buildings with five or more units. Always call the broker to respond to specific ads; don't call without having something specific to discuss. Do not pinch the sales commission, which will be paid by the seller. The broker will earn his commission by handling the details of the transaction and by negotiating a better deal and securing better financing than you might on your own.

If you run across a property you are interested in and there is keen competition to snap up the property, the property is probably not for you. This is especially true if it is one of your first investments in real estate. Competition often pushes the price too high. This was certainly the case during the run-up in property prices from 2003 to 2006. And we all saw how that turned out.

The main mistake you can make is paying too much. The winner of a competition to buy property will almost always pay more than necessary. In almost all cases, you do not want property that people are rushing to buy. The preferable properties are the not-so-attractive, money-losing properties that are sometimes priced low because they have been on the market for a while. Unimaginative investors are not interested in these properties, but they can be real bargains if you take the time to evaluate them carefully.

Chapter Recap

Consider the following when negotiating with brokers and sellers:

- In any building that you contemplate acquiring, consider the existing tenants.
- Consider the existing unit mix and the future tenants you can expect.
- Be careful in evaluating the current net income that any building produces.
- Decide ahead of time the ways in which you can increase the present income.
- Before making an offer, decide the maximum that you can pay and the lowest that the seller might accept.
- Often, competition to buy properties can push the price up beyond what is necessary.

-4-

====

Financing Your Acquisitions

Investment decisions or personal decisions don't wait for the picture to be clarified.

—Andrew Grove, executive

When buying real estate, you make money by going into debt. I know that sounds backward, but it's true. This chapter will show you how and why that statement is true. It begins with knowing how to structure your monthly payments carefully. Here is a quick example of how this works. If you buy a property and then upgrade it, you can increase the rents. At this point, your payments for financing should be no more than 45 percent of the scheduled gross income of your property. If your expenses are 35 percent, this automatically gives you a 20 percent profit on rents. Though you owe money on the property, you are still making a 20 percent *profit* on it.

In this chapter you will learn to use debt and leverage wisely and to maximum advantage. But first it is important to understand the terminology involved. Most people understand what debt is, so we'll skip ahead to leverage. Leverage is using borrowed money to finance investments. Even if someone can buy a property free and clear, he can choose instead to structure the deal to limit his cash outlay. Successful investors use a smaller proportion of their own money and a larger proportion of other people's money. This increases the overall return on their money, and it also reduces risk. In short, they are using other people's money to leverage their own investments. The most important thing to remember is to be sure that you don't get overextended. Only commit to monthly mortgage payments that the property will support; that is how you win the leverage game.

In the post-financial-crisis environment that we operate in today, funds for real estate loans are scarcer than at any time in the recent past. It pays for you to be aware of additional methods of financing that can help your expansion. Below is a list of a dozen ways to borrow money. All of these methods will undoubtedly become more popular in years to come.

- First trust deed
- Subject to
- Second trust deed
- Seller carryback trust deed
- Create a trust deed
- Blanket trust deed
- Wraparound trust deed
- Contract of sale
- Commercial loans
- Subordination agreements
- 100 percent financing
- Lease/option

Most of these methods will illustrate how you can acquire real estate for the smallest down payments. These unique financing methods will allow you to use as little of your own money as possible. Let's break it down.

First Mortgages and Deeds of Trust

The type of loan on which you can get the best terms, the lowest payment and interest, and the longest repayment period is the first mortgage or deed of trust. The term *first mortgage* designates the loan that is the first recorded lien against the property.

Your first option should always be to finance through a first mortgage, whether you are seeking funds for improvements or for other purposes. To finance most improvements, many investors look to second loans, which come with higher interest and payments and create additional liens on the property. Make it a habit to try securing the most favorable terms through a new first mortgage.

Many state laws favor the deed of trust over the mortgage for a real estate loan. Either type of loan may be used on a first or second lien. A deed of trust is designed to give greater control to the lender. For example, state laws permit completing a deed of trust foreclosure in four months, while a year is necessary to foreclose a mortgage. Trust deeds are often referred to as mortgages, as both are considered recorded loans against real estate, but a trust deed is not mortgage.

Most likely, any of the properties you will be looking to purchase will already have a first mortgage on it. In all likelihood the loans will represent between 30 and 80 percent or more of the proposed purchase price.

The methods of financing described here primarily concern filling the gap between your proposed purchase price and the amount of the existing mortgages already in place. In most cases you will need between 3 and 25 percent of the purchase price for down payment. I will illustrate several methods of financing the purchase price beyond the existing loans on the property, especially when you don't have the down payment to obtain a new mortgage loan. When you are applying for conventional financing, institutional lenders normally require that you have at least 25 percent of the purchase price as a down payment. They might require more if the current cash flow would put the lender in a risky position.

Subject To

The term *subject to* involves having the seller deed you the property without you obtaining a new mortgage or trust deed. The buyer makes the mortgage payments on the seller's existing loan(s) but does not take out a new loan to make the acquisition. Basically no financing is required. You simply take over the responsibility for making the payments on the loan that is secured by the property that you are buying. As illustrated in chapter 6, this offers you the opportunity to repair and upgrade the property and adjust the rents before you apply for a new mortgage. In most cases you will be able to obtain a larger loan at this later date because of the increased income from the property.

Most mortgage loans have a "due on sale" clause. This means that the mortgage documents include a provision that requires the mortgage or trust deed to be paid in full (or allows the lender to call the loan due in full) if the property is sold or transferred. When you get the deed, the lender can demand full payment of the loan. However, if the lender is getting on-time payments from you, it is unlikely to institute an expensive and time-consuming foreclosure. But you need to know that it can happen, especially if it is a low-interest rate loan and the rates begin to go up.

This type of financing should be treated as only a temporary solution to your financing needs. I have used it to buy time to increase the value of a property with the intention of refinancing in order to pay it off shortly after, usually within two years.

The alternative to taking a property subject to the existing loan(s) is to formally assume any loans on the property. This means you put the loan(s) in your name. However, this requires you to put in a substantial down payment. It is the same as if you were to take out a new mortgage or trust deed. You will also need to pay the lender a fee of around 1 percent of the principal loan balance in closing costs. It is better to upgrade the property and increase the rent it produces before applying for a new loan. In this way you can almost always get a larger loan that will better meets your needs.

It is important to understand that some properties you contemplate buying will not qualify for new loans. In other words, the lender may not like the appearance of the property, or there may be other mitigating factors. In many cases lenders do not like to make loans on neglected property, which is understandable. Why loan on risky collateral? This happens often on income property where good management is essential for success.

So, in taking over a property subject to its existing loan, always be prepared to refinance in the very near future. You need a plan to pay off any loans that are not in your name or the name of your entity.

Second Deeds of Trust

Second deeds of trust, or second mortgages, are used frequently to fill the financing gaps between the first loan and the proposed purchase price. Sometimes referred to as junior loans, most are short-term, meaning they are usually designed to be paid off in three to five years. Often the regular monthly payments are not big enough to pay off the debt during the term of the loan. Therefore, there will be a balloon payment due at the end of the term.

Often these loans are paid off by refinancing with a new first trust deed. This is very feasible if you have owned the property for a couple of years, made improvements to the property, and increased the rental income. Commercial banks, credit unions, finance companies, and even private individuals are potential sources of funds for second mortgages. Second mortgages are commonly used, for example, when you have a 15 percent down payment and are able to obtain a new first mortgage at 75 percent of the purchase price. The remaining 10 percent to be financed can be obtained through a second or junior trust deed. This financing is normally referred to as 75-10-15. Conventional lenders can arrange this type of financing when you are lining up a purchase. Usually it is done only on properties consisting of one to four units. Lenders normally do not make second loans on larger apartment buildings or commercial properties.

A second deed of trust is a subordinate (junior) claim on the property and may be a second, third, or lesser one. You cannot tell the position of the liens just by looking at the actual note because it does not stipulate a first mortgage, second mortgage, and so on. Usually the priority depends on the date on which each trust deed was recorded at your local county recorder. When your abstract, or title company, does a title search they will determine what claims each deed of trust has against the property and the priority of each.

Primary and *secondary* are two words you will hear often in real estate dealings. When real estate people talk about financing, primary financing means loans secured by first trust deeds or mortgages, and secondary financing is a loan that has a secondary or subordinate claim against the property.

Second loans are made all the time in the buying and selling of income property. They are made to facilitate sales by making up the difference between the buyer's down payment and the amount of any existing loans on the property that are being assumed or taken subject to by the buyers or the amount of the new loan that the buyer may be placing on the property.

If an investor/seller needs to take back a second deed of trust to facilitate a sale, he or she can then offer the trust deed as partial down payment on another purchase. In other words, if your deed of trust is well secured on a good piece of real estate, you can use it to expand your holdings. Normally someone accepting your deed of trust would like to see that it is "seasoned," which means that it has been on the property and has been paid on for at least six months. In this day and age, some lenders want it to be seasoned for a year or more.

Also, in the event you need to raise cash for whatever purpose, you can sell the trust deed that you took on your recently sold property to another investor. If this is the case, you will need to take a substantial discount to do so. This is done to increase the attractiveness of the overall return to the person buying the trust deed. Since a second lien is considered a somewhat risky endeavor, investors compensate for this by bumping up the expected return.

As your dealings in real estate expand, so will your knowledge of second trust deeds.

Seller Carryback Loans

The seller of the property that you are buying can sometimes be the best source of financing. A seller can *carry back* a first or second deed of trust or mortgage to facilitate a sale. Selling is likely to be more important to the seller than to any lender. If you are the only prospective buyer, it is definitely to the seller's benefit to work out something with you.

If the seller's property is rundown and in need of some management, he would probably take a lower down payment and lower interest rate in addition to carrying back a mortgage. Another advantage to you with a carryback loan is that the seller would probably hate to have the property foreclosed on, which gives you an open door to negotiate. If you ever end up in need of a payment schedule readjustment, it is more than likely that such a seller will consider working something out with you.

In your early discussions with either the seller or the broker handling the sale, you will learn about the seller's desires. You may learn, for example, if the seller needs a large amount of cash from the sale or mainly wants a steady income for her retirement years. The seller's tax position could also be an important consideration.

You would be surprised at how many elderly owners like to take carryback mortgages on their properties to provide them with some kind of monthly income. If the owners no longer have the desire or ability to maintain the property, they could be open to the possibility of creating a first or second mortgage for you to help facilitate a sale.

It is up to you to negotiate for such an arrangement. Normally the seller will need to feel secure that you will make the payments regularly and on time. Both you and the broker will need to convince him that there will be no problem in doing this. Sometimes the seller may ask for a larger down payment or some sort of security on another property that you own. This is something I will come back to shortly.

A carryback loan should always be offered to an owner who may be selling because he wants to be relieved of property management and maintenance responsibilities. Carryback loans are especially useful if owners already have substantial equity in their properties. Many sellers like to receive good return on their principal and may agree to being paid off five to seven years in the future.

Creating Mortgages or Trust Deeds

Okay, let's say that you have found an apartment building that you would like to acquire. While negotiating to buy the property you find out that your money is tight. You've been unable to get a new first or second mortgage on property that you already own that would have provided the cash necessary for the down payment for your new purchase. The seller wants to sell you his property, although he is finding that buyers like you are also having difficulty coming up with the down payment. He wants to work with you to solve your problem.

Creating a second mortgage or *trust deed in favor of the seller* of the apartment building may be the solution. In other words, the seller might be willing to let you buy his property on credit. This benefits you as it saves you from going through a lending institution to get cash to cover your down payment to the seller. You'll also avoid a loan fee, as well as other costs of the transaction. You and the seller will negotiate which of your properties to put the new trust deed on, as well as the interest rate and terms of the loan. Any title company can help you write up a promissory note and deed of trust. Upon completion of these items, they can advise you on how to have your trust deed recorded at the county where the prospective property is located.

Obviously, you are much better off this way than you would be if you converted part of your equity in your own property into cash by taking out a new first or second trust deed through a private lender or mortgage company.

All of this boils down to one big question: Would an owner of an apartment house consider taking a second trust deed on a property you already own instead of a cash down payment? In many situations the answer is yes. Tax considerations can influence an owner. Some owners have management problems that they do not want to deal with. Or they may simply be tired of managing the property. If their apartments need extensive repairs, owners may feel that they are better off selling the property. The owner may feel that, if he wants a large cash down payment, he will need to substantially reduce his price. Besides, a well-secured second mortgage can be a worthwhile investment for the seller.

A created mortgage can help you fill the financial gaps between the purchase price and existing financing on the property you want to acquire.

You may hear realtors and investors also refer to creating a mortgage or trust deed as cross-collateralization. Basically you are giving the seller of the property you want an interest in a building you own. Given a choice, many sellers would rather take the trust deed on a property that you have had for some time than give you a second trust deed on the building that you want to buy from them. It could be that the seller may feel more secure in the fact that you have "seasoning" if you have owned your property for a while. It may be that your building is in better condition than the property that he is selling to you. You will need to prove to the seller that you have equity in the property that you want to put the trust deed on. This can be accomplished by showing the seller any appraisal you may have had done recently along with a mortgage statement that indicates the outstanding balance of the loan on the property.

The created mortgage can be paid off when you refinance the property a few years down the line, after completing some timely renovations to increase the value of the property. Obviously, this solution only really comes into play once you have multiple investment properties to work with. Regardless, it is something to keep in mind.

Blanket Mortgages

A loan covering more than one piece of property is usually referred to as a *blanket mortgage.* This is used to extend credit beyond the ordinary limits that can be obtained by financing properties individually. The lender spreads his risk by having one loan for multiple properties, which often justifies heavier financing. Blanket mortgages may be first or second loans, or a combination of both. The same mortgage might be a first on some properties and a second on others.

Let's look at how a blanket mortgage can help you as you expand your income property holdings. You have applied for a new first trust deed on a property that you have recently renovated and where you have increased the rental income. The lender that you are dealing with indicates that your new rent schedule is really not seasoned enough. In other words, your new rents have recently been raised, and there is not sufficient history to project the future. At this point you can offer to secure the new trust deed on the subject property and another that you own.

Now, if the lender agrees with your proposal (and many bankers will), you may ask that the banker agree to release your property offered as additional collateral from the blanket mortgage when the net income reaches agreed-upon goals, usually in two or three years.

Completion of other tangible objectives can also be used to release the property put up as additional collateral. Some of these objectives might be the completion of specific improvements, such as painting the exterior or replacing the roof.

Be sure to put such release agreements in writing, otherwise your banker or seller might be unwilling to release property from the mortgage, or might hold you up for a big payment before he will do so. Using a blanket mortgage is a good way to sweeten a deal, provide additional security for your banker or seller, or help when you are short of cash.

Let's say you own five or six properties that have recently been refinanced with new first mortgages. You want to expand your holdings, so you locate a property that has potential if you make some improvements. In negotiating with the seller, you find that you need additional funds to complete the financing and to make a down payment. Approach your bank and request a blanket second mortgage to secure what you need in additional financing. It may be that no one property of yours will satisfy the bank's equity requirements, but a blanket mortgage covering all of your properties would be appropriate.

Blanket mortgages are often used in subdivisions. A subdivider may blanket a block of lots under one mortgage or might build several houses under a blanket construction loan. A release clause is usually included as part of the loan terms providing that a piece of property may be released from the blanket mortgage upon a stipulated proportionate payment; this permits the builder to sell individual properties.

Wraparound Loans

A *wraparound loan* is sometimes referred to as an overriding trust deed. It is a junior deed of trust that includes the unpaid balance of all existing trust deeds that are senior to it on the property. A wraparound is generally used for a sale or, less frequently, for refinancing.

For example, to start with a simple wraparound, Owner A sold an apartment house to Buyer B, taking back a $400,000 all-inclusive, or wraparound deed of trust at 7 percent interest, subject to an existing bank loan of $280,000, which carries interest at only 5.25 percent.

Owner A was comfortable with receiving interest at an annual rate of 7 percent while paying out interest at 5.25 percent. The difference between the underlying loan and what Buyer B paid monthly was thus 1.75 percent, and Owner A is able to pocket the difference.

It worked out for the buyer too. He avoided the loan origination cost he would have incurred if he had taken out a new first mortgage.

This option is also a good one if rates on new first trust deeds exceed what the buyer is willing to pay.

To maintain a wraparound deed of trust, you must be certain that

- loan payments are made on time;
- taxes are paid when due; and
- insurance is paid when due and continues to be issued in the names of the original lender and original borrower.

An all-inclusive note is best when there is no acceleration clause in any of the mortgages against the property.

When there is no clause to block them, wraparound loans can be good to use if certain criteria are met:

- There is a loan in place that has a substantial prepayment penalty.
- The buyer is making a small down payment.
- The property is overpriced, and the seller sticks to the price but not the terms of sale.
- The existing loans are at lower interest rates than you could get on new financing.
- There is little time to shop for a new loan, and the down payment is so low that the only alternative is for the seller to carry back a large purchase money mortgage.

The wraparound loan became popular when interest rates rose in the 1970s and through the 1980s. The purpose was to sell or refinance real estate without having to pay off or increase the interest on an existing low-interest-rate loan. This is another form of seller financing, which in this case allows the seller to profit somewhat from a below-market interest rate on original loans placed on the property.

The fact is that due to today's low-interest-rate environment, the wraparound loan has not been utilized much. This may change in the near future as our economy begins to expand and interest rates begin to rise. Lenders would never admit it, but wraparound loans can help them because multiple parties are interested in ensuring that loan payments are made on time. Each party is protecting its own equity interest in the property. The two parties (or more) that are involved can set up a collection account to handle only the loan payments, or they could also include a monthly proration of taxes and insurance. At any rate, Buyer B needs to ensure that the original owner (Owner A) is making all underlying loan payments to prevent foreclosure on the property.

When interest rates rise, the wraparound loan can benefit both the buyer and the seller, especially if buyers do not want to place a high-interest-rate loan on the property, which would decrease the net income from the property.

Contracts of Sale

Also referred to as a land contract or contract for deed, the *contract of sale* is used as an alternative to wraparound trust deeds. In both types of financing, the buyer pays the seller, who is still responsible for payments due on existing mortgages against the property.

One important difference between the two is that, with a contract of sale, the deed is not transferred. Possession of the property—but not the deed—may be delivered to the buyer. A buyer entering into a contract of sale must wait until the conditions of the contract are fulfilled in order to acquire the title, but in the meantime he does become an equitable owner of the property with rights of possession. This transaction is normally used for two purposes: to avoid disturbing existing loans and to offset the buyer's lack of money or credit.

A contract of sale may or may not be recorded. Sometimes the deed may not be transferred until the seller is paid in full, but the usual practice is to deliver the deed after a certain amount of money is paid—usually a substantial portion of the seller's equity.

A contract of sale is a good tool to use when the buyer has a small down payment. The seller simply retains the deed until the buyer meets his obligations. The contract of sale gives the seller greater control when the buyer has little money to put down. The buyer's objective is to complete property improvements, and increase income within the allotted time in the contract. In most cases, if the buyer's objectives are met, a new first trust deed can be completed. The buyer would then pay off the seller and receive the deed to the property.

Here's an example: A fourplex was sold for $210,000, with only $6,000 down. The contract stipulated that the deed would be transferred when the seller was paid his equity in the property. The contract of sale payments were set at $1,020 per month, the same as for an interest-only loan payable at 6 percent per annum.

The existing first mortgage of $165,000 was payable at $885.76 monthly, including 5 percent interest. During the term of the contract the seller was responsible for the monthly mortgage payments. This old loan would be paid off when the buyer refinanced with a new mortgage.

I'm including here a copy of an old contract of sale that I have used in the past. This method is further illustrated in chapter 6. A more detailed land contract can be found in Appendix B.

CONTRACT OF SALE

This contract, made and entered this [date] by and between _____, hereinafter referred to as Vendor and _____, hereinafter referred to as Vendee.

WITNESSETH, that the Vendor agrees to sell and convey, and Vendee agrees to purchase.

All that certain plot, piece of parcel of land, with the building and improvements thereon erected, situated, and being in the address known as

_____.

LEGAL DESCRIPTION: Attached as Exhibit A.

IN CONSIDERATION THEREOF, the Vendee agrees to pay to the said Vendor the sum of $_____ per month beginning [date] through [date]. In addition, the Vendee agrees to repair and renovate the property.

TERMS AND CONDITIONS:

Upon the execution of this contract the Vendor will no longer own the marketable and equitable title to this said property. The Vendee will own the equitability of the said property. The term of this contract will be for a thirty-two (32) month period. There is no prepayment penalty on this contract. The Vendee owns the accumulated equity in the property and can retrieve the equity at any time. The principal sum of this contract is the existing 1st mortgage balance plus $_____. This principal sum shall be due and payable on or before [date].

TYPE OF DEED TO BE CONVEYED: Grant Deed.

Vendor agrees to surrender possession to Vendee on or before [date].

_____

Vendor

_____

Vendee

Commercial Loans

Commercial loans, usually obtained from a bank that you have developed a relationship with, can be quick sources of sizable amounts of cash. Building your credit will influence your speed of expansion. It can provide funds for emergencies and help pay for annual expenses, such as taxes. Having such credit available forms a cushion, which enables you to invest with less cash in reserve than you would otherwise. Standby commercial credit is almost the same as ready cash. Your financial statement can increase your ability to obtain commercial credit.

Interest usually compares with mortgage rates. Where it differs from mortgages, though, is that the loan is normally arranged for a specific period. Some are made for six months or maybe a year—so the payback is short. At the end of the term, the full principal is due.

Sometimes the promissory note (the amount you have borrowed) might be renewable upon its expiration date, but at least the interest should be paid. Renewal would receive favorable review if some of the principal is paid—for example, $5,000 on a $30,000 note. Notes may be renewable several times. However, banks do not like extensions exceeding one year. Some businessmen renew their commercial loans year after year, but seldom pay them off. Make a practice of paying off notes or credit lines in full when they are due, even if you might have to request a new loan within a month or two.

Besides protecting against emergency, or seasonal financial needs, the commercial loan can be used to complete purchases and improvements, pending receipt of long-term funds. The commercial loan can help fund your property improvements until you obtain a new, larger, long-term first mortgage. When the new first mortgage completes your refinance, the excess funds can repay your commercial credit line.

A variation of the commercial loan could be a property improvement loan, which many banks can give without collateral. A commercial credit line is normally available to an income property owner as stand-by credit for business purposes. However, an improvement loan is normally for the specific purpose of enhancing property value. Usually the term for an improvement loan is short (you need to pay it back sooner rather than later). Also, interest rates can be high—higher than a commercial line of credit—but lower than credit cards.

This is but one more method of borrowing funds for real estate. I would say a commercial credit line is essential for your success, so you should try to get one as needed. However, keep in mind that improvement loans are normally short-term, expensive options.

Subordination Agreements

Subordination agreements are used most often in land sales where the buyer intends to improve the property with new construction. In order to grant a construction loan, the bank would require that the buyer's deed of trust to the seller of the land be subordinated to the bank's new first trust deed. An example would be a homebuilder who purchases a lot from a private party. The builder makes a down payment of $20,000 on a $100,000 purchase price. He proposes to the private party that he (seller) carry a first deed of trust for the balance of the purchase price, which in this case would be $80,000. The builder/buyer also asks that a subordination agreement be included with the first deed of trust securing the $80,000 note. If the deal is completed as proposed, then the builder can immediately obtain a construction loan, subject to the lot seller subordinating his trust deed to a new first-trust-deed construction loan.

An income property owner can use subordination agreements when raising funds for improvements, paying down a second trust deed, or partially paying off the seller's equity. If, for example, you owned a property that had a $300,000 first trust deed, a second trust deed for $200,000, and a value of $750,000, you could ask the holder of the second deed of trust, in the absence of an agreement, to subordinate to a new first trust deed of, say, $375,000.

You could offer inducements to the holder of the second trust deed to convince him to subordinate. Such inducements might include the following:

- Higher interest
- Larger payments

- An earlier due date
- Reduction of the principal

If the proceeds of your new mortgage will be used to make improvements to the property, you should be able to substantiate an increased value upon completion. This will provide additional security for your second trust deed holder and add an extra incentive.

Remember, the best possible loan you can get on income property is a new first trust deed. Normally it is the lowest interest rate you can obtain as well as the longest term (usually thirty years). However, the maximum loan-to-value (LTV) that a mortgage will provide on income property is 70 percent, so the loan amount is somewhat limited. Whenever there is a possibility of financing through a first mortgage, you should explore that option first.

In the above example, you, as the owner, would net $75,000 on the mortgage put in place, provided the holder of the second trust deed subordinates. This can be used for improvements on the subject property or to complete the purchase of another building.

So if you own a property and are making payments on one or more mortgages against it, you can normally refinance it with a new first mortgage that pays off the existing loan or loans as part of the transaction. If not, your new loan will not be a first mortgage; it will be a second, third, or fourth, depending on how many other loans are already outstanding against your property.

As mentioned earlier, you want to keep the lower interest and longer term of a first mortgage. But the only way you can get a new first mortgage without paying off all of the existing loans against the property is to persuade the holders of the existing loans to subordinate them. They must agree in writing that the new lender will get paid off before they do, if you default on your debts.

Ideally it is much better to postpone trying to get a new first mortgage until after you have completed the improvements. By doing so you establish a higher value for the property and therefore are in a better position to get a new loan and pay off all the liens on the property. However, sometimes this is not possible, so subordination remains an option for getting the funds to improve and modernize the property.

I know this is a lot to chew on, so let me summarize the main points to keep in mind when considering subordination: When you take on a second mortgage, try to get the lender to agree to subordinate if you refinance with a new first mortgage. Most lenders probably will not agree unless there is some incentive for them to do so. Incentives can be a principal paydown on their loan, a higher interest rate, or completion of property improvements that will increase the value of the property. Increased value adds equity that better protects the loan. Another point to keep in mind is that, unless you have no alternative, you should postpone refinancing a rundown property; you can get a better loan after you increase the property's value by doing improvements.

If you are an experienced investor, the subordination methods described above can provide you with the cash to quickly complete substantial property improvements or acquisitions. But if you are new to investing, I would encourage you to avoid borrowing in the beginning to make repairs and improvements. If you are buying income property that makes sense financially, you should be able to pay for improvements from the net income that the property produces. If you are rehabilitating the interior, for example, you can do one apartment at a time. You can finance the improvements from income you receive on the other rented units. This will also force you to shop for handymen who can help you complete your projects for the least money. You should start on another apartment only after you have rented the completed units. When starting out, remember that babies don't run marathons. Smart planning and execution will make all the difference in the world.

You should set aside reserves for large projects, such as a new roof, exterior painting, or new water heating systems.

What about 100 Percent Financing?

People buy with nothing down all the time, but don't expect to do it often. If you have patience and persistence and can recognize the right situation, you can buy a property and pay only closing costs—or maybe no money at all.

No-money-down terms are not advertised. Sellers and brokers are not likely to mention that the down payment could be waived. Most sellers expect a reasonable amount of cash. The only reason a sale might be entertained would be to get cash for another real estate purchase or other purpose. The seller would also have to pay a sales commission and other expenses tied to closing costs.

Even if you prove to an owner that you have been investing successfully in real estate for a long time, have plenty of assets, and possess a good credit rating, the owner is still likely to prefer selling to someone who will make a down payment. Often his only reason for selling is to get his hands on some cash.

But there are some exceptions. Some sellers do not need cash. Other sellers have let property run down so badly that a no-cash buyer usually is the only kind who is interested. Many sellers yearn to free themselves from the work of managing their properties.

Distress situations can offer opportunities. If an owner is overwhelmed or operating at a deficit, he may be mainly concerned about cutting his losses. He may pass up the down payment to get the problem off his hands.

Buying without cash will depend heavily on your ability to ask for and negotiate for such terms. One common opportunity for a no-money-down purchase is an income property in which the seller has a large equity. You might suggest that the seller refinance the property before selling it to you; he would receive the cash he wants with no immediate liability for taxes on any cash he receives. Then he might be able to sell to you on a contract of sale. Again, this can work when the seller has substantial equity in the property.

It is not necessarily good business to buy in this way. It would be a bad idea to commit yourself to unrealistically heavy monthly payments. You need to be extremely confident that you can refinance the property in a few years for enough cash to pay the seller's note. This can be done if you are able to improve the property (as discussed in the next two chapters) to substantiate 30 percent (or more) additional income from the property. This would enable you to get a new long-term 70 percent mortgage, which would provide the money to pay the seller's equity. The benefit for you would be that you will have paid the seller's equity and created a 30 percent-plus equity in the property for yourself.

As a buyer, you may make the seller more comfortable by putting up additional collateral. If you have sufficient equity in another property apart from what you are negotiating to buy, you could offer a trust deed on your other property to add additional security. In this way you have created enough extra security that the deal could be worthwhile to the seller.

One hundred percent financing can also mean that you borrow all the purchase costs, putting in no money of your own. Many people who do not have cash in the bank arrange for 100 percent financing by getting a 75 percent mortgage loan on a property and then borrowing the other 25 percent elsewhere. Many people with steady incomes can get personal loans from finance companies, credit unions, or banks. Someone can also borrow on his or her home or some other security. If one succeeds in borrowing all necessary funds through such arrangements, this can be considered 100 percent financing.

Now for a quick word of caution. If you have taken to heart the principles set forth in this book, you should be able to use leverage safely. Analyze any potential transaction so thoroughly that there will be little risk of any lender foreclosing on you. Your financing will be structured in such a way that there will always be more than enough cash flowing in to meet the debt payments you have signed up for. And do not forget to include all of the expenses associated with running the day-to-day operations of the property.

Lease/Option

I have had more success with this method of private financing than any other. Rather than immediately buying the property, you enter into a *lease and option* to purchase the property with the prospective seller. Granting someone an option to buy, however, is not the same as signing an agreement to sell, but it can be considered a conditional sales contract. An option promises to hold an offer open for a period of time. The prospective buyer puts up consideration (usually money) to maintain the option. Other considerations can be the lease itself. You could consider the option a long escrow period. In the meantime, you lease the property and make monthly payments equal to or larger than the payments the seller is obligated to make on the mortgage. The term of the lease/option I have had the most success with is between three and five years.

When you enter into the lease, the seller gives you an option to buy the property any time during the term of the lease. This also relieves the seller from the day-to-day management of the property. In many cases this is the seller's sole motivation for selling. Be sure to agree on the option price before you enter into the deal. In the meantime, of course, the buyer is responsible for property taxes, insurance, improvements, and maintenance. Plus, the buyer pockets the difference between all rents collected and all expenses paid during the term of the lease. There are several examples of this method of financing in chapter 6, "How to Buy Income Property."

Again, as with a contract of sale, the buyer's objective is to make property improvements to increase the rental income and property value so that in a few years the buyer can refinance to pay off the seller's equity and obtain the title to the property. As in all of these examples of alternate financing, the buyer's goal is to create at least a 25 percent equity in the income property.

For your protection a memorandum of option to purchase should be recorded with your county recorder. The benefit of the lease to the seller is that he or she is free of all expenses associated with the property. Option to purchase agreements automatically lock in the seller's equity. The seller is in essentially the same position as if the property had been sold and carried back a trust deed.

This is one more solution to the problem of a down payment that a buyer feels is too big. Often the same seller who demands a $100,000 down payment will settle for a $50,000 payment as a lease security deposit or consideration for granting the option to buy and let the prospective buyer lease the property. It can be useful to both the buyer and seller.

There can be variations to the above as well. For example, I once had an apartment house seller grant me an option to buy his building, but he did not want to lease it. We worked out a deal whereby I made the repairs and improvements, refinanced the property, and eventually exercised my option to buy. The deal benefited everyone involved.

All of these financing methods work, given the right situations. As you gain experience, you will learn to recognize opportunities in which various methods would apply to your situation. Some great examples can be found in chapter 6. I have used each and every one of these methods, but I must point out that not every realtor or broker that you come into contact with will know of these seller-financing strategies. In certain circumstances, no doubt, you will need to educate your broker and seller. Rest assured, this book will always be here for you to reference.

Chapter Recap

In this chapter, we identified various creative financing methods to help make acquisitions and improvements.

- Usually your best source of financing is a first trust deed or mortgage.
- Consider asking the seller to carry back a loan for the difference between your down payment and existing loans on the building.
- When you only have a small down payment, consider offering a contract of sale or lease option.
- After you upgrade the property and increase the rents, your mortgage payments should be no more than 45 percent of the scheduled gross income.

-5-

═══════════

Improvements and Operations That Make You Money

Success ... seems to be connected with action. Successful men keep moving. They make mistakes, but they don't quit.

—Conrad Hilton, hotelier

Population growth and inflation both contribute to increasing property values, but you cannot depend on them over any specific period of time. You have to make improvements to your property to increase its overall value. This idea is the keystone for how to make big profits from small properties. Take for example an apple. You can buy an apple for a dollar, but if you try to sell that apple for two dollars, you probably won't get many takers. Now, if you spend two more dollars on some sugar, flour, butter, lard, and spices, you can turn that simple apple into a pie. You've invested three dollars to make the pie, and now you can sell that pie, a slice at a time, for five dollars a slice. It is a general example, but you can better understand the concept here. Improvements are essential to your success in making your property yield more income and increase in value. Seldom will property hold a consistent value, as all buildings are subject to depreciation.

You do not want to be an owner who bleeds potential income on a property by not spending on improvements. An owner may be forced to revise rents, pricing them lower because of increasing vacancies. This owner may come to a point where he cannot meet expenses due to lower rents and shoddy, deteriorating properties. As a rule, rent continues to increase for well-maintained rental units, while deteriorated properties normally undergo rent decreases. However, these situations normally create bargains for buyers who are willing to make improvements, as you will see in the next chapter. The imaginative investor realizes a far more dependable income and can earn a substantial gain when he sells or refinances down the line. Improvements increase both income and resale profits.

There are two major methods of improving property: physical change and improving the appearance of property; and improving management operations.

Physical improvement covers painting, updating design and fixtures, and landscaping. We will cover this first.

What Improvements Should I Make?

Making money on improvements will be reflected in selective buying. But you should concentrate on upgrades that can increase value at minimum expense. You want to make your property as desirable as possible. The best rule to follow as a property owner is that your property should represent what you would want if you were operating on the budget of the average prospective tenant. If you wouldn't live there, why would anybody else?

In the buildings you acquire, your objective will be to upgrade not only the physical appearance of the building but also the type of tenant that will be attracted to your property. You want to attract quality tenants who will have pride in where they live. You need to provide clean, modernized, and up-to-date places to live—in all of your units. If you accomplish this on a broad scale you have a good chance of obtaining a higher income for yourself, better tenant relations, and overall peace of mind.

However, you should keep in mind that overimprovement may actually be more *unprofitable* than underimprovement, as you can easily price the unit out of the rental market. Try to stay within your neighborhood level. Be careful about installing items like trash compactors and dishwashers, especially in neighborhoods where other rental units do not currently have them. From an investment standpoint, in the average rental unit, these types of upgrades might cost more than they would repay.

You will find that the most practical examples of value-producing improvements are new carpets or hardwood floors, modern kitchen cabinets, up-to-date countertops with stainless steel sinks, bath vanities with new sinks, and ceramic tile bath and kitchen floors. Installation problems for these features are usually minimal. Other profit-making options include painting; replacing obsolete, worn-out electrical fixtures; changing plumbing or heating fixtures; landscaping; and installing window blinds.

Examples of not-so-profitable upgrades include replacing the roof or repairing or replacing the foundation. Normally tenants will not pay more in rent for these repairs. You cannot blame them for expecting a dry roof and stable foundation; yet repairing these items takes priority over, say, installing a new kitchen sink or floor. The same goes for a new water heating system for the building you own. Needless to say, tenants expect hot water and will not pay more for it.

You are probably better off negotiating the cost of these types of repairs from the purchase price with the seller. There is little opportunity for retrieving your cost from getting increased rents for these types of repairs or additions.

Permits

You should inquire about permit requirements in your particular city before beginning many types of improvements or repair work. In general, you can do painting and landscaping work without city inspections. The point of most permits and required inspections is to make sure the work is done properly. For example, heaters or tubs would require inspections to see that water, gas, and vent connections were properly installed. If there is any question of improper installation of the work, the inspector will point out the changes necessary to pass inspection.

Under most circumstances, pulling the necessary permits is the responsibility of the contractor when you sign the contracts. If you are doing the work yourself, you need to get the required permits yourself. Permits are usually required when making permanent alterations to a building, such as rewiring or adding a room to a structure.

Improving the Exterior

Exterior painting probably will provide you with the greatest return. It is amazing how many owners neglect to paint their buildings. After all, the exterior is the first thing prospective tenants see, and it should be high on the list of improvements.

Anyone—even someone without experience—can do a first-class paint job. With a little care, you can save about two-thirds of the average contractor's charge. You or your handyman may choose to do the first two stories of, say, a three-story building. It is advisable, though, that you have a professional painter do higher work. They are experienced in handling ladders and working from higher places. If you are concerned about your workers' safety—and you should be—do not hesitate to hire professionals to complete your job.

Try to pick modern, up-to-date colors for your exterior. These color blends change just like clothing fashions. Your local paint store can help you with color schemes.

A darker base (usually stucco or wood siding), complemented by a lighter trim, can make your building look bigger. Conversely, if you want your building to look smaller, reverse the above and place a lighter color on the base and a darker color on the trim. The current trend is to use a trim color of white or off-white with a darker base.

You should apply a coat of primer before you paint. The finished paint will look so much better and will last longer as well. There is no need to take shortcuts, as a good, well-prepared exterior paint job can last fifteen or more years.

When you are finished, do not forget to add new brass house numbers. As I said, the first thing a prospective tenant sees is the outside of your building. Good features such as well-placed windows and doors can be emphasized by contrasting colors.

Landscaping

Many owners neglect to install a lawn, or if there is one, they fail to keep it up. According to appraisers, neat, well-kept landscaping can add as much as 10 percent to the value of your building. There is no doubt you will also attract a better-quality tenant with attractive landscaping.

Any landscape gardener will make a plan for your garden area for a given fee and specify the plants and shrubs you should use and what will look best in your area.

If you have a large area in front of your property, normally a green lawn can be used to cover it most efficiently. It certainly looks better than concrete. Before laying the lawn out with sod, you should probably think about installing an underground sprinkling system. Don't expect an apartment manager to take the time to consistently water the lawn and move the hose and sprinkler head around your yard. Take the time and expense to install an automatic sprinkler, as it will pay for itself in the long run. Your lawn will last much longer and look much better. Don't forget to hire someone to cut the grass. Your manager or someone you hire can cut the lawn every two weeks.

Windows

If you are using the methods I recommend, the properties you acquire are likely to be fifty to seventy years old. In most cities, almost all apartment income properties were built many years ago. As a result, the windows have more than likely deteriorated, and judging from my own experience, I would suspect that they probably were not well designed in the first place. New vinyl, double-pane windows are very attractive when viewed from the outside. Also, new windows today are energy efficient and very functional from the tenants' perspective.

Attempting to repair older windows can be frustrating. Parts are often hard to find, and wooden windows often have substantial dry rot. This is a situation in which a repair job can be a significant improvement. Local glass or window companies can now install new retrofit double-pane windows with screens in less than one hour for a standard size. New, updated windows should be a must if you are looking for a good, effective upgrade.

Interior Improvements

Electrical systems and plumbing should always be checked before you start any remodeling work. If you have low water pressure in the shower and sinks, for example, you will more than likely need to replumb these items with copper piping. If this is the case, get several bids from plumbers and choose one that you are comfortable with. If you are working on an apartment house, you will likely have this problem throughout all of the units. Tell the plumber you can give him additional work in the building as the units turn over, and he might give you a multiunit discount.

In almost every apartment, at the very least, you will need to replace worn-out electrical receptacles with new up-to-date, three-prong receptacles. The same goes for light switches. You should replace them with newer, silent switches. Even push button switches and outdated hanging fixtures make dwellings look ancient, and they can generally be updated quickly and easily, which will benefit your property as a whole. Outdated fixtures should be replaced unless you consider them desirable antiques and you plan to advertise them as such. Also check to be sure there are adequate electrical outlets in each room; this is a must in the tech-savvy world that we live in.

After checking for the above, begin work on remodeling the apartment. For the next few pages, I'm going to refer to an interior remodel that I completed on a very outdated property that I owned. This is not a step-by-step instruction manual, because every situation is different; it is more of a shining example of how to overhaul the interior of a property to increase its value. At the end, I'll even show you a cost breakdown (see Figure 2) of the work I completed so you can measure the costs out of pocket against the potential profits of higher rents and higher property value. Again, this is only an example of what I do, and I take no responsibility for any problems that you may run into with your interior remodel.

Once the work is completed for basic electrical work upgrades and any replumbing, it will be time to focus on the bathroom and kitchen.

The bathroom will probably be outdated, with decades-old fixtures, walls, and flooring, and the kitchen may still have a cast-iron sink and old, worn countertops.

In a unit like this one, I begin the work by turning off the water. (In multifamily buildings, you should give your tenants at least twenty-four hours' notice that the water will be turned off.) Next, I dismantle the existing kitchen and bathroom sinks by starting with the water supply lines that connect to the faucets. I remove the old wall-mounted sink in the bathroom. If the existing toilet is old and uses three and a half gallons of water or more per flush, I make plans to replace it with a low-flow (1.6 gallon per flush) toilet.

In the kitchen, I remove the old material that served as the countertop. I've seen both tile and old Formica. I remove the old cast iron sink. Sometimes the sink is attached permanently to an old metal sink base cabinet. In this case, I simply remove the entire sink and sink base cabinet. As the saying goes, "Out with the old …"

After the above items are disconnected from the walls, I replace the water angle stops, often referred to as shut-off valves, with new ones. The old ones often leak, especially when you hook up new water supply lines.

In the bathtub and shower, I remove the shower stems and shower diverter to check their condition. Sometimes they simply need new washers. But if the handles are old and discolored, it pays to simply replace the stems and install new handles. Unfortunately, you will find that plumbing is not very standardized. Often you have to replace one component with entirely new kits to get things to fit properly. In other words, you may not be able to find new handles to fit your old stems. Electrical work, however, is very standardized, so you will not have these kinds of problems as often.

After everything is disconnected, I install new shut-off valves under the sinks in the bathroom and kitchen. I replace the angle stop that serves the toilet as well. Next I install new shower and diverter stems and new chrome handles in the bathroom.

Doing this work yourself is not difficult or too time consuming, and it is a cost-effective way to increase value. If this is above your skill set, you can contract the work out, but in many cases, a good book or the Internet can lead you step by step through how to do this type of improvement to your property.

When these jobs are completed, I turn the water that serves the building back on. At this time, I check for any leaks that the new additions may have created. To minimize any inconvenience to my tenants, I ensure that the new angle stops and any other materials that I plan to use are at the job site while the water is shut off. It pays to always be prepared in advance.

It is good to remember that these types of jobs should be done during the middle of the day when tenants are not likely to need their water. These are the details that you should be aware of if you are overseeing the job. You will need to be the person to give notice to the tenants of their upcoming inconvenience. Most plumbers and handymen are concerned mainly with getting the job done and are not very concerned with the inconvenience that the people in the building may experience.

Before installing a new bathroom vanity and sink, new toilet, and new kitchen sink and countertop, I always make arrangements to paint both the bath and kitchen walls and ceilings. You should plan on two coats of semigloss paint. Normally, an off-white color is best. Whatever color and type of paint you use, it should be the same for all of your units. Maintenance is much easier when you use similar paints for all of the interiors of your apartments.

At this time I arrange to have all old carpets (as well as the old sinks, cabinets, countertops, toilets and old plumbing parts) lifted and hauled off the property to the dump.

After painting the bath and kitchen, and hauling away debris, I begin the prep work in the bedrooms, hallways, and living rooms. The walls and ceilings should be cleaned with a degreaser (trisodium phosphate, called TSP) to remove all accumulated dirt and grease. Next, I patch up any holes and cracks with spackling paste or joint compound. After the filler material has thoroughly dried, I sand these areas to provide a smooth finish. When they are smooth, I spot prime these areas so that it will not show through the finish coat.

In order to get the job done in a timely fashion, I do the necessary prep work to spray paint the bedrooms, dining room, living room, and halls. I cover the windows with paper and masking tape. Also, I cover doorknobs and heaters appropriately. The details are important.

I usually decide on a good-quality flat latex paint to cover these areas. In almost all cases, I have found that it is best to choose an off-white color for the apartment interior. Normally, a paint sprayer will apply enough paint to make a second coat unnecessary. Of course, before applying a finish coat, any walls painted a dark color need to be primed so the dark color does not show through the light finish coat. This is a decision I make on a case-by-case basis. If I don't need primer, then I just choose an off-white flat finish. Again, my intention is to use the same brand and color of paint in all apartment interiors. Small imperfections can lead to huge problems down the road.

I have found that an average-sized apartment, excluding kitchen and bath, can normally be spray painted in less than two hours. This saves a tremendous amount of time, and in most cases the finished paint job looks much better than if I just rolled the paint on. The sprayer applies more paint to the walls and makes it look more evenly spread.

The next day, I check to ensure that the paint has completely dried. I then clean up and remove all prep and masking materials.

At this time, I arrange to have the finish materials for the bath and kitchen delivered. For the bathroom, I get a new vanity with a sink, a faucet, water supply lines, a toilet, towel bars, and a shower rod. I apply new floor tiles or linoleum at this time.

The kitchen job is a little wider in scope. I install ceramic tile for the floor; this requires installation of a subfloor to which the tiles can adhere. This job can take one person up to five days to complete. When completed, the floor should look better than applied linoleum and probably will last longer.

Upon completion of the kitchen floor, I install a new laminate countertop, stainless steel sink, and new faucet over the existing sink base cabinet. If a new one is needed, premade sink cabinets are available in various sizes at most building supply stores. All you need to do is paint them, if necessary, and attach them to the kitchen wall. It is pretty easy once you get the hang of it.

After the work described above, I begin to install new light fixtures, where necessary, throughout the apartment. This small upgrade can pay off in big ways. I also cover the new light switches and electrical outlets with new plates.

At this point, it has been about ten days since I completed the interior paint project. Since then, I have also finished installation of the new bath and kitchen items. The last couple of things I like to install are a new medicine cabinet in the bathroom and new closet panel doors in the bedroom.

At this point, I put a "for rent" sign at the front of the building, as the apartment is acceptable to show. I completed an extensive renovation, remodeling the kitchen and bath, and added a fresh coat of paint along with new wall fixtures. In less than a few weeks' time, I have created a new apartment experience. But I have one more thing that needs to be done: flooring.

First off, I measure for installation of padding and carpeting. An average one-bedroom apartment takes about fifty square yards of material. If you purchase your carpet goods at a home improvement outlet, they can normally cut the sizes that you will need for each individual room. You need to work with twelve-foot-wide carpet material, because this is the only way it comes. Don't worry—you learn to make it work with experience.

If your handyman has plenty of experience in installing carpet, he can complete the job in one day. His work will include wall-to-wall installation, seaming the carpet, and putting on the carpet bars.

As a final touch, I always install new entry door locks (including a dead bolt) and new interior doorknobs throughout the apartment.

Finally, the renovated, remodeled apartment is complete. In the last few pages, you have read what I do to my newly acquired units. This work helps me tremendously in getting a better-quality (and better-paying) tenant.

Following is a list of materials (Figure 2) that you will need to complete an apartment as described above. The retail prices are typical of what you would pay at your local home improvement store. As you can see, doing it yourself can save money up front, and the upgrades will make a world of difference when completed.

Figure 2: Ready Materials List

Materials	Estimated Cost
Kitchen ceramic tile and backerboard	$300
Six-foot countertop — laminate	$62
Stainless steel kitchen sink	$108
Kitchen faucet	$68
Sink strainer	$10
Bath sink and vanity	$145
Bath faucet	$58
Shower handles(kits)	$110
Toilet	$98
Bath linoleum	$75
Carpet for average apartment, fifty square yards	$700
Light fixtures, receptacles, and cover plates	$85

Operations That Make You Money

The objective of successful management operations is to improve the net income on your property. Your goal is twofold. First you want to increase the gross income by increasing rental value and eliminating vacancies. At the same time, you want to decrease operating expenses. Most of the former will be obtained by doing the improvements. To ensure your success in producing increased net income, consider the following:

- Pay close attention to property assessments to be sure you are not overpaying on property taxes. Most counties have an appeal procedure.
- Always monitor your insurance policies. Cut coverage that you think is too high. Obtain bids on your policies from different companies. You will be surprised at how competitive insurance companies can be.

- Make it a habit to monitor interest rates. It is sometimes advantageous to refinance your mortgages with lower rates. This applies even if you are not taking out cash. The difference in monthly payments can be substantial.

- Install low-flow showerheads and faucet aerators, and rebuild leaking toilets. The biggest saver is replacing large-tanked, 3.5- to six-gallon-per-flush toilets with low-flow (1.6 gallons per flush) toilets. Some water municipalities will reimburse you for the cost of each new low-flow toilet you install.

- If you have a laundry facility on your property, install front-load washing machines. A front-load machine uses substantially less water than a top-load washer.

- Work out a plan with your local waste management company regarding the most efficient way to handle refuse collection at your property. Also, encourage your tenants to recycle. Often you will find money-saving ideas if you do the research.

- Finally, keep your tenants happy. Respond quickly to maintenance requests. The cost of finding new tenants is time consuming and expensive. Keep your property neat and free of litter and always be looking for ways to improve the appearance.

When you do have turnover, maintain productive advertising and salesmanship to fill vacancies and minimize rent loss.

Realize that all income properties can stand a close look to improve operations. A capable individual owner will almost always outperform a bloated property management company. Do not get me wrong—there is a place for management companies. There is a huge demand for their services. You may even choose to hire one. But keep in mind that they usually charge between 5 and 10 percent of the gross rental income. Variations depend on the size and location of your property. You should also know that your vacancy factor and maintenance expenses will be considerably higher than they would be if you applied your own individual effort.

When you acquire a building, it does not pay to blindly follow the practices of the average former owner. The former owner may be selling because of declining revenue and generally poor operating methods. In the next chapter, "How to Buy Income Property," you will see that you can improve the net income by improving upon the previous owner's operating methods. Many times, the inefficient operating ways of the former owner were satisfactory to him. This may be because he had a large equity, lack of pressure to increase the income, or generally a lack of knowledge. This offers plenty of opportunity for you, the enterprising investor, to expand and improve, all to your benefit.

When you are starting your investment program, you should work to obtain management experience by doing it yourself. Numerous organizations can help you with this. Local or county Apartment House Association branches are common for this. There are also state and national apartment associations that exist to help individual owners and ensure the benefits of private capital that is invested in rental housing. They keep up with proposed and current legislation that may affect your operations. They have sources that advertise for your business. This would include handymen, plumbers, roofers, and carpenters, as well as places where you purchase appliances and other materials. Wholesale buys on everything you need to operate your apartment house are available through local associations. Even when legal counsel is required, local associations can direct you to attorneys that specialize in any problems you may encounter,

On-the-job experience in running apartments can be invaluable in eventually directing individual managers to run your operation. But even if you start out doing it yourself, you eventually want to delegate all of the physical labor to others as your experience and property holdings increase. The same can be said for property management as a whole. Putting the day-to-day operations in someone else's hands will allow you the opportunity to look for acquisitions and still generally oversee your apartment operations.

Your main goal in this endeavor should be to avoid vacancies. You want to keep tenants longer and rent to new tenants seamlessly without long lag times between tenants for any given unit. To meet these objectives, you should

- maintain your building's neat and attractive appearance;

- add improvements that tenants desire; and
- try to keep rents within a moderate price range and at fair market value.

Even with judicious implementation of the above points, realize that you will experience a certain amount of turnover. It comes with the territory. A worthwhile objective is to keep your vacancy factor under 3 percent. Filling your occupancies quickly will reduce your vacancy factor and is one of the best ways to increase your net income.

The most important factor of all is ensuring that your vacancy is adequately advertised. Prospective tenants need to be informed through your advertising.

The following are several methods that owners employ to get the word out on their vacancies.

Vacancy Signs

Your local signage shop can make a very durable, informative, and colorful sign that should be posted in the front of your building. I know of apartment houses that keep mostly full by using nothing but vacancy signs. These should be located on or near major streets where there is a good deal of traffic. Most owners draw at least some of their tenants by using signs.

Newspaper Ads/Associated Internet Sites

Most prospective tenants usually glance through classified ads, looking for essential information that meets their housing needs. Then they phone the listed numbers to seek additional information. Because of this, you should not include every single fact about the apartment. The color of the walls in the living room has no bearing during this part of the process. It is important to include enough information to get your prospective tenant interested in your opening. If there is interest, they will reach out to you.

To avoid heavy expenses associated with newspaper classified advertising, you need only mention the most important features of your vacancy, including the following:

- Number of bedrooms
- Price per month
- City in which the vacancy is located
- Specific neighborhood
- Phone number to contact

The above can be put into two lines, thereby reducing your cost. The best days of the week to run the ad are Thursday through Sunday. Be sure that your newspaper runs the ad on its associated websites. According to various newspaper outlets, approximately 50 percent of your prospects will come from this source. Make yourself, or your manager, available to answer the phone during the days on which your ads run. Failure to do so will create a huge missed opportunity.

During your eventual telephone conversations, try to screen your prospects. Some will simply be shopping, and others will be seriously interested in your vacancy. In time, you will learn to tell the difference.

Many prospects will make appointments to see the vacancy. A few will not show up. Do not take it personally; this is the nature of the business.

Finally, if you have many apartments, ask your local newspaper if you can receive discounts for frequent ads. Most newspapers offer these discounts, though in most cases, they are not advertised. You should also set up a monthly billing account to smooth your operations.

Use of Flyers

Posting flyers in the community can be a way to let people know of your vacancy. Use PowerPoint to produce flyers in color, with interior and exterior photos of your vacancy. Emphasize the location, size of the apartment, important (or sell) features, and price. Try posting your flyers on community message boards and at bank branches, local churches, neighborhood markets, youth sporting event venues, and similar places in the neighborhood. An attractive flyer will at least encourage people to look at it, and if they look at it, they may pick it up and pass it along to someone they know. Catching the eye of a potential tenant is very important here.

Word of Mouth

It helps to cultivate friendly tenant relations. Sometimes it may be appropriate to reward one of your existing tenants monetarily if they refer a successful applicant. Often, if leaving for reasons other than dissatisfaction, an outgoing tenant will make an effort to obtain a replacement. The more you do for your tenants, the better the return may be in the long run.

Internet Listings

Craigslist.com and other similar advertisers are worthwhile places to list your vacancy. These sites are free, and you can post photos. Take some time to research which websites have a good level of daily traffic and a history of making connections between sellers and buyers. The Internet is your friend.

Real Estate Broker

Real estate brokers can be very effective, especially in renting vacant houses. Many tenants pay commissions to real estate brokers for locating houses to rent.

Most business leases and corporate housing leases are handled through brokers. You will find, though, that most apartment vacancies can be filled more quickly, and more efficiently, by using the methods I describe rather than real estate brokers. Hiring a broker is an option, but it should be near the bottom of the list.

Section 8

In your continuing search for tenants for your vacancies, you will undoubtedly be asked by a prospective tenant, "Do you accept Section 8?" This will be especially true if your apartments are located in moderate- to low-income neighborhoods. Following is a brief overview of the federal government's Section 8 program.

From time to time, the government issues housing vouchers to US citizens and to specified categories of noncitizens who have eligible immigration status. In general, the family's income may not exceed 50 percent of the median income for the county or metropolitan area in which the family chooses to live. The public housing authority in your area must provide 75 percent of its vouchers to applicants whose incomes do not exceed 30 percent of the area median income.

The federal government's Housing Choice Voucher Program assists very low-income families, the elderly, and the disabled to afford decent, safe, and sanitary housing in the private rental market. Since housing assistance is provided on behalf of families or individuals, participants are able to find their own housing, including single-family homes and apartments.

The participant is free to choose any housing that meets the requirements of the program. A family that is issued a housing voucher is responsible for finding suitable housing of the family's choice where the owner agrees to rent under the program. Rental units must meet minimum standards of health and safety, as determined by local public housing authorities.

A monthly housing subsidy is paid to the landlord directly by the local public housing authority on behalf of the participant. The family then pays the difference between the actual rent charged by the landlord and the amount subsidized by the program. The tenant's portion of the rent is limited to 30 percent of his income. The balance is paid by the local housing authority, via the housing subsidy given by the federal government.

Federal housing assistance programs began in the 1930s during the Great Depression. The Section 8 subsidy program was created decades later by the Housing and Community Development Act of 1974. It allows very low-income tenants to rent and lease market rate apartments at fair market values. What constitutes fair market rent is established by the local public housing authority. This figure is established by tracking open market rents for one-, two-, and three-bedroom (or larger) apartments and houses.

The greatest advantage in working with tenants that have Section 8 vouchers is that the portion paid by the government is guaranteed. Also, the local housing authority can act as a buffer between you and the tenant. This helps to ensure that the tenant's portion of the rent is paid. In most cases, these vouchers are good for a lifetime, and a tenant does not want to jeopardize losing Section 8 status by not paying their portion of the rent or not obeying your house rules, thereby risking eviction.

When you accept a tenant on Section 8, you will be asked to fill out a government form entitled "Request for Lease Approval." The prospective tenant will take this paperwork to the housing authority and arrange for an inspection of the premises. In order to pass, your apartment or house will need to be in tip-top condition. Some owners complain about this requirement, but your units should be in outstanding condition anyway. This is especially so if you are following the advice in this book. If you choose to accept Section 8 tenants, you should ensure that your apartment passes on the initial inspection. This provides for good relations with your tenants and the housing authority, and it helps reduce your vacancy factor. You will realize soon enough that most initial inspections of other landlords fail. This means the tenant cannot move in immediately and the inspector has to schedule another appointment while the owner completes repairs. If you plan on going with Section 8, it would be best to make sure your units are in the best condition possible.

When the unit passes, you will sign a one-year lease, which becomes month-to-month after the first year. The tenant is responsible for the deposit and any other fees you charge at move-in.

In my area, the Section 8 rent is started on the day after the unit passes inspection; however, it normally takes up to three weeks to receive your first check.

The local housing authority performs annual inspections on the units leased to them. Any needed corrections or repairs must be completed within thirty days. If the repairs are not completed in the allotted time, your lease is subject to cancellation. If this happens, you lose your subsidy, and you will no longer be paid. Do not let this happen, as you will be left to evict the tenant on your own.

My overall experience with Section 8 has been very good. About 20 percent of my units are rented this way. On the first of every month, the local housing authority wires the lump sum amount for all my Section 8 tenants directly to my bank account. There are no late payments and no rent collections to do for those portions. I am able to make all my mortgage loan payments for the subject properties from this source.

However, in choosing tenants for this program, try to choose the ones who have jobs and sources of income. Normally, they will make for better overall tenants than those who are not employed.

As with any government program, you must allocate a burdensome amount of paperwork and attention for units rented under this program. But if you are committed to maintaining your apartments, and you like guaranteed rent that is automatically deposited in a lump sum on the first day of each month to your bank, you should consider incorporating Section 8 into your operation.

Lastly, most housing authorities located in large cities maintain a newsletter where you can advertise your vacancies.

What about Rent Raises?

In order to increase your operating income, you must raise rents from time to time, and certainly when it is economically feasible. It is not uncommon to find that rents in desirable older properties are considerably lower than the going rates. They can sometimes be raised immediately or when the current leases expire.

Historically, rents have increased along with tenants' incomes and operating costs such as taxes, utilities, and repairs. In your inspection of properties, if rents have stayed the same for a long time, this can be attributed to the property not being as well maintained as it should be, or it could be because of the present owner's reluctance to institute rent increases. He might fear losing tenants. Normally, increases of 3 to 5 percent are not regarded as excessive by tenants, many of whom have increased their own incomes considerably. The best time to raise rents by more than 5 percent is upon apartment turnover and when the unit becomes vacant. Market rent becomes feasible at this time.

There are fewer complaints and fewer terminations of occupancy when rents are raised after improvements are made, because you have then established a tangible increase in value.

Another typical time to raise rents is with the announcement of higher costs, which tenants expect to have offset by higher rents. In your letter to tenants regarding rental increases, you might explain the higher expenses of taxes, gas, electricity, and maintenance and repairs.

You need to give at least sixty days' notice of increase. The effective dates are usually best near the beginning of the new calendar year.

On Section 8 tenancies, you need to apply to the local housing authority to request an increase. Normally they will compare your requested amount to market rents in the area. I normally apply each year for an increase. My experience is that increases for some tenants are approved while others are not. In many cases the increase is paid by the government, and the tenant's portion of rent is not affected.

Chapter Recap

You can increase the worth of your property by two methods. One is to improve the property's physical appearance. This includes improvements such as the following:

- Interior and exterior painting
- Renovating landscaping
- Installing new windows
- Updating kitchens and baths
- Installing new carpet or hardwood floors

The second method is to improve management, or the management operations. There are a number of ways to do this, including the following:

- Closely monitoring property expenses, especially utilities
- Minimizing rent loss by reducing the vacancy factor
- Not blindly following the practices of the former owner
- Raising rents from time to time and when feasible, especially after making improvements

-6-

How to Buy Income Property

Business opportunities are like buses. There's always another one coming.

—*Richard Branson, entrepreneur*

The opportunities to find and purchase viable income properties are out there—you just need to know where to look. The key is to find the *right* income property for you and your goals. To begin on this long and exciting road of finding that *right* property, your objective should be to find sellers with any of these characteristics or scenarios:

- Unimaginative owners who have allowed their properties to deteriorate
- Multiple heirs who let property decline because none of the owners have taken responsibility
- Disagreements within partnerships, especially over who is responsible for costs or operation and management
- Older owners who wish to liquidate and take back mortgages

Keep these points in mind as you inquire about various properties. As per chapter 2, by now you probably have investigated several neighborhoods and are starting to narrow your search.

You stand a better chance of finding success if you hold to the simple rule of asking, "Is it good enough for me?" When looking at potential properties, ask yourself that question. Owning and improving a property that you would choose to live in if you were on the same budget as prospective tenants puts you in their shoes and allows you to see the endeavor through their eyes. Remember, being on a budget does not always mean being low-income or cash-strapped. If you stick to this rule, you will stand a greater chance of financial success. Though you are buying and refinancing property, it is the people that truly matter.

So look for properties that you would live in. This does not mean "slumming it" or "living beneath your means"—it is just a commonsense rule. Some properties could be brought up to a whole new class or standard with simple upgrades like those mentioned in the previous chapter. Because of this, you can look for properties in many different types of neighborhoods. Low-income neighborhoods offer the best chance at rehabilitation, but the return may not pay off at first. Well-to-do neighborhoods may never pay off as the lifeblood of those communities is normally tied to the economy. That leaves moderate neighborhoods or, like the story of the three little bears, neighborhoods that are "not too hot, and not too cold, but just right." These types of communities are where you should focus first.

Also, properties in marginal neighborhoods often pay the greatest return for the money invested, but they may offer little opportunity for capital gain and enhancement. However, making improvements where, as in many cities, an entire area is undergoing rehabilitation should be profitable.

As previously mentioned, you will need a down payment of between 3 and 25 percent for most acquisitions. So, for the moment, let us assume that you and I have saved $15,000 from our wages to use for income property investment. These funds may be used for a down payment on the purchase price and/or to make improvements to the property. The examples below offer a detailed chronicle of actual income property buys, incorporating the fundamentals from previous chapters. This is where we start to bring it all together for a practical purpose. Remember, in this example, we are starting with $15,000 in cash and a newspaper. So let us begin.

Finding Your First Income Property

We begin to investigate the purchase of properties for sale through newspaper advertising and the Internet. After several weeks of searching we run across an ad for the Drake Apartments, a fourplex located in a part of town that has some new construction going up. We call the broker, and he advises us that the owner is anxious to sell but wants an all-cash deal. We learn that the rent for each unit is $450 a month. The only utility paid by the owner is garbage removal. Water service is individually metered and paid by each tenant. Each apartment has its own water heater as well; this means the tenants pay for their own hot water—a big plus. The estimated value of the building is about $175,000.

Upon arrival at the Drake we notice that new condos are actively being sold on the opposite corner from the building. This is always a good sign. We also note that the property is close to employment centers and near all area freeways for easy commuting. The property is older and of a 1940s construction style. Also the building is small for a fourplex, only about 2,500 square feet total. Most residences in the area are single-family homes that appear to be much older than the subject property. In all likelihood, sometime during or after World War II, an older home was torn down, and this fourplex was erected in its place. We notice very few "for rent" signs in the neighborhood. This too is a good sign.

The property itself looks neglected. The small double-hung windows throughout the building look deteriorated and rotten. Wooden stairs that lead to the upstairs units look to be very old and suffering from dry rot. The roof appears to be nearing the end of its useful life.

We conclude that a new buyer will have to do a substantial amount of deferred maintenance. We also recognize that it would be difficult for the owner to obtain an all-cash sale because there would be too much out-of-pocket expense for the buyer to fix up the building. Few buyers are willing to risk a large down payment *and* fix-up costs unless the price is exceptionally low.

We call the broker and set up a meeting at his office. He tells us that the owner bought the property from an institutional lender that had foreclosed on the property after the latest recession. He states that the owner has tried to operate the property for income, but his partner has not done a good job. It turns out the seller is a speculative homebuilder whose projects are some distance from the Drake. The broker arranges for us to meet the seller's partner and inspect the units.

Upon inspection, we note the following issues and review them with the broker:

- Two units are vacant.
- All units have worn and older carpet.
- All the units need new paint.
- All of the units need new kitchen countertops, new linoleum, and new sinks.
- All of the units need new bath vanities and sinks, subfloors, and linoleum.
- There are no showers over the bathtubs. (Inexpensive overhead showers can be installed for the convenience of the tenants, but we keep that to ourselves for now.)
- In the very near future, most of the wooden sash windows will need replacement.

Making the Deal

Now comes the fun part. The negotiating back and forth in any real estate transaction resembles a tennis match, with both sides lobbing the ball back and forth until finally a point is scored and the deal is done.

We meet with the broker and tell him that, in lieu of the down payment, we want to invest heavily in property improvements. We tell him that we estimate it will cost about $15,000 to renovate the property, so our upper limit purchase would be $90,000. He says he will discuss it with the seller and get back to us, although he says that the offering price is absurd.

In the meantime we check comparable sales in and around the neighborhood. We note that several fourplexes have sold in the range of $150,000 to $180,000. The rents for the Drake Apartments are low when compared to the rents in these other properties. After renovation we estimate, based on comparable rents, that we can increase the rents in this building to $800. We can only get this much from new tenants, as this would be too much of an increase for the two existing tenants.

To summarize:

The Drake Apartments		
Monthly Income before Renovation	$450 × 4 = $1,800 per month	
Expenses		
Garbage	$85.00 per month	
Taxes	$130.00 per month	
Insurance	$63.00 per month	
Monthly Net Income		$1,522.00
Annual Gross Income		$21,600
Less 5 Percent Vacancy Factor		- $1,080
Adjusted Gross Income		$20,520
Taxes	$1,560	
Insurance	$756	
Utilities	$1,020	
Maintenance (Est. 8 percent)	$1,728	
Total Expense	$5,064	
Current Net Income		$15,456

For most purchases, it is necessary to estimate maintenance expenses. The national average is 8 percent of the gross income. Sometimes the seller's expenses may not be what you would spend, depending on whether the seller does his own work or contracts the work out.

Based on rents in the area, we can estimate net income after we complete the renovation:

The Drake Apartments		
Annual Income ($800 × 4 × 12)		$38,400
Less 5 Percent Vacancy Factor		- $1,920
Adjusted Gross Income		$36,480
Expenses		
Taxes	$2,000	
Insurance	$756	
Utilities	$1,020	
Maintenance (Est. 8 percent)	$3,072	
Total Expenses	$6,848	
NEW NET INCOME		$29,632

The renovations, together with rental increases, represent an approximate increase in net income of 100 percent. The numbers point to this as a solid investment!

We can see that this is a good buy, provided the seller will entertain a reasonable offering price. Due to the circumstances, we deduce that we may be the only buyer interested, so we can raise our purchase price somewhat from what we have offered, if needed.

Remember, the overall goal is to increase the capital value of investment property, after improvements, by at least 25 percent. In this case we estimate the cost of improvements to be $15,000. The purchase price we estimate will be $95,000. So purchase price and the cost of improvements would add up to $110,000. Judging by the comparable values in the neighborhood, we estimate that the value of this property, after improvements and upgrades to the building, will be about $175,000. (We arrive at this value by using the neighborhood comparable sale method discussed in chapter 3. This represents a gross profit of about $65,000—nearly 37 percent! Seeing as this is well over the target of 25 percent, we have room for error in estimating the finished value or the cost of the improvements. Again, we feel we are onto a profitable purchase.

The broker calls and tells us that the seller cannot accept anything less than $115,000. The seller realizes that at this price he would be selling well under the potential value, but he is very motivated to get out of the partnership. In order to bring the purchase price down, we explain to the broker the improvements that are needed and the cost. This is part of the game.

The broker goes back to the seller and outlines our position. He counters our offer at $100,000, with all cash to the existing loan at closing. We immediately counter at $97,000, with a $3,000 down payment and the stipulation that the seller is to cover the balance in a second deed of trust. Now the ball is in his court, as the saying goes.

One week later we hear back from the broker. He tells us the seller accepts the offer with one stipulation of his own. He will carry his equity in a second deed of trust but wants to be paid off in two years. This does not allow us much time to complete the improvements to the property and refinance it to pay off the seller.

Again, we go back to our numbers and our estimates. Since two of the four units are vacant we can assume that these units will be rehabilitated rather quickly. For the other two units, we will need to wait for tenant turnover in order to renovate. Over two years we can expect at least one of the apartments to open up, as is the industry average. That would give us three fully upgraded units (out of four total) with higher rents, which would help us achieve the goal we are looking for.

The broker indicates that if it takes longer than two years to pay off the seller, he would extend the note, but at a higher interest rate. We decide we can accept these terms.

We agree to this stipulation and ask if we can put the sale agreement in the form of a land contract or contract of sale (see chapter 4). Using this method we can save considerably on closing costs. The seller agrees to this, as the terms benefit him at present. The deed will stay in his name until we pay off his note, and we agree to make monthly payments to the seller in the amount of $1,100 per month. From this amount, the seller will make the underlying loan payment on the first trust deed; any remaining balance will pay a return on the seller's equity in the property. We will be responsible for all other expenses associated with operating the property, including insurance, utilities, property taxes, maintenance, and improvements. We will also be responsible for collecting rent and choosing tenants.

The income and expense obligation that we have signed up for looks as follows:

Monthly Gross Income		$2,500
Less 5 Percent Vacancy Factor		- $125
Adjusted Gross Income		$2,375
Expenses		
Taxes	$130	
Insurance	$63	
Utilities	$85	
Maintenance	$220	
Total Expenses	$498	
NET INCOME		$1,877
- Less Loan Payment		- $1,100
NET INCOME IN-POCKET		$777

These obligations are well within the projected income of the property. However, included in the monthly income above are the new rents on the two soon-to-be-renovated apartments. We project that these two vacancies can be completed and rented within the next four months, which fits our rule that the property should be making money after six months of ownership. The numbers add up in our favor, based on our goals, so we are ready to proceed.

Out of our initial $15,000 savings, we put $3,000 down and arrange to close our land contract at the end of the month. We time it this way so we can collect the rents due on the first day of the following month. We are able to operate with these rents because the seller's note payments do not begin for thirty days. In other words, rents are due in advance, and interest is normally paid thirty days later. These prorations are important to know and understand, especially on larger income properties. Rents due on the first of the month plus tenant security deposits can help you pay fees and closing costs on the pending deal.

So now we have a contract, and we own the property. The next phase of ownership is to begin the renovation on the two empty apartments.

At this point we can do the work ourselves if we have both the time and inclination (see chapter 5). The benefit of doing the work ourselves is to not only save money at the beginning stages of our investment but also to place a solid monetary value on the work completed. This will make us more knowledgeable when discussing bids with contractors and handymen, now and in the future.

There are many sources for locating contractors and handymen should you choose to contract the work out, not the least of which would be newspaper advertising and local real estate offices. Normally, obtaining three bids will be sufficient for your purposes. While this is not a concrete rule, I've found that three bids is a good sampling of what is out there. Three separate bids usually provide enough information for you to make an educated decision and to hire someone trustworthy to do the work.

Now we can move on to the next objective. So far we have located a good buy, negotiated a profitable deal, and begun the remodeling process on two of the units. At this point we should act with some urgency, knowing we need to complete the improvements and increase the rental income in order to obtain a long-term, low-interest first trust deed on the property.

The seller stated that he would carry his note for longer than the two years we agreed upon, but we can facilitate a sale or trade up much more easily if we have a long-term, low-interest *new* loan in place on the property. As explained in chapter 4, your best and cheapest money will come from a new first trust deed from a financial institution. This is the safest loan anyone can make, provided the lender stays within reasonable loan to value (LTV) ratios.

We have advanced our handyman the money to purchase supplies and complete the renovation of the two empty apartments. Now it's time to advertise and obtain new tenants.

Upon completion of the remodeling, we agree to rent to two Section 8 (see chapter 5) tenants. The rent that we are able to obtain is $750 on each apartment—a little less than our desired goal of $800 per month but still within our financial parameters.

After we rent the two empty units, the occupant in apartment A gives notice that she will be moving in thirty days. We plan to renovate this unit and then rent it at the higher rent.

Within forty-five days of our original tenant's move, we rent the newly rehabbed unit for $800 per month.

We have now owned the building for fourteen months. We decide to seek refinancing with a new first mortgage in our name. We apply at a local bank that makes income property loans in our city.

We present the following income and expense statement to the loan officer who will facilitate our loan.

The Drake Apartments		
Monthly Income/Expense		
Monthly Gross Income		$2,750
- Less 5 Percent Vacancy Factor		- $138
Adjusted Gross Income		$2,612
Expenses		
Taxes	$130	
Insurance	$63	
Utilities	$85	
Maintenance	$220	
Total Expenses	$498	
NET INCOME		$2,114
- Less Existing Land Contract Payment		-$1,100
NEW NET INCOME		$1,014

The Drake Apartments		
Annual Income/Expense		
Annual Gross Income		$33,000
- Less 5 Percent Vacancy Factor		- $1,650
Adjusted Gross Income		$31,350
Expenses		
Taxes	$1,560	
Insurance	$756	
Utilities	$1,020	
Maintenance	$2,640	
Total Expenses	$5,976	
NET INCOME		$25,374
Contract of Sale Payments	$13,200	
Net In-Pocket		$12,174

We submit a copy of our original contract of sale to the loan officer and provide her with a list of the improvements that we have made over the past fourteen months. She checks our credit to make sure it is sufficient and then orders an appraisal on the property.

A week later we get a call from the appraiser. We arrange to meet him at the property and give the tenants twenty-four hours' notice that the appraiser will need to enter their apartments. We explain that it is for a brief inspection and that he will need to take some measurements.

When the appraiser arrives he notes that three of the units have updated kitchens, baths, paint and carpet. He also notes that the community is growing quickly with a good deal of activity and that renovation is ongoing throughout the district. He writes in his report that the area is an older, established neighborhood and an easy commute to the downtown area, local shops, services, and public transportation. These are all points that we noted when looking for the property in the first place. That bit of research in the beginning is paying off now.

The appraiser notes that loan discounts, interest buydowns, and sales concessions, except for payment of nonrecurring closing costs, are not common at this time in the area. Growth rate and property value have remained stable over the past year, although sales have recently picked up because of the relatively low interest rates and the strength of the economy. (I want to stress again that this is just an example; this information is tailored to show you how the information in this book would come together on an actual deal. I hope that, after reading this chapter, you will understand how this works.)

Final analysis of the appraisal is that the value of the property is $160,000. The comments on final reconciliation are that the sales comparison analysis was considered the best indicator of value as it best reflected the actions of buyers and sellers in the two- to four-unit residential income market. The value of the property was further supported by the income and cost approaches to value.

So our ballpark estimate of value upon completion of improvements—$150,000 to $180,000—was fairly close to the appraiser's analysis. Keep in mind that appraisals are hardly a science but simply an opinion of value at a given time.

Normally income property lenders will make a loan to property value of 70 percent. In this case we could expect a loan in the amount of $112,000, that is, 70 percent of the appraised value of $160,000 ($160,000 × 0.70 = $112,000).

However, the lender tells us that, since we have only owned and operated the property for fourteen months, we do not have sufficient seasoning (as previously mentioned, two years' worth of records is the norm). Because of the lack of seasoning on the property, the loan officer explains that the loan will have to be cut back to the balance owing on the contract of sale plus closing costs. In this case the principal amount of the new loan will be $100,000.

Upon analysis we decide to take this new first trust deed loan for these reasons:

- We can pay off the seller's short-term loan.

- The property deed will be conveyed to us.
- We will have in place a new long-term loan that will make selling the property easier if we choose to do so.

The loan helps to establish a gross profit of 30 percent on our purchase and improvement costs, that is, the $97,000 purchase plus $15,000 improvement costs. At this time the property cash flow is providing net income of about $1,000 per month. Again, that is *net income*, which is profit that we make after all obligations are met.

For the moment we decide to continue to operate the property and save the net income for our next opportunity. We also intend to complete improvements in the remaining apartment once it becomes vacant.

Several months pass and our one remaining occupant puts in a notice that she intends to vacate in thirty days. In the meantime we have repainted the front of the building and replaced the old address numbers with new brass numbers and fixtures. The simple procedures can pay huge dividends, as explained in chapter 5.

After renovating of our last apartment, we rent it to a new tenant for $800 per month. We continue to hold the property and are now getting approximately $4,200 more in annual net income. In a little less than two years' time, and starting with a fund of $15,000 in savings, we have turned those savings into a profitable business venture. But, wait—there's more!

Buying Your Second Property

One evening we get a call from the same broker that sold us our initial fourplex. He is happy that his commission was paid when the seller received his loan proceeds from his contract of sale.

He gives us the address of the Cypress Apartments, a five-unit property, which he thinks we may have an interest in purchasing. It is located on the other side of town. We tell him that it may be out of our way, but if it's an exceptionally good bargain we will give it our best shot.

We drive out to the property to do a quick visual inspection and notice that there is an older two-bedroom house in the front with a 1960s-style fourplex at the rear of the property.

The house is vacant and has several broken windows. The broker explains to us that these tenants had to be evicted because of several large dogs that they were keeping. It looks like the dogs did quite a bit of damage in and around the property. We also inspect one vacancy in the fourplex. We notice that the kitchen and bath are in original condition and would require modernizing in order to get better tenants and rents. The carpets and linoleum are in poor condition and appear to be at least fifteen years old. The broker tells us that all of the units are in similarly poor condition.

Additionally the broker tells us the seller apparently does not have the wherewithal or desire to fix up the property. He only owes $89,780 on the property, and it produces net income for him because his payments and taxes are so low. He gets by on the low rents. The asking price is $220,000.

In order to fix it up and raise the rental income, we figure we will need a budget similar to what we had in place for the Drake Apartments. We spent $15,000 modernizing the apartments at the Drake, plus the $97,000 purchase price. As mentioned, in view of the $160,000 new appraisal, we turned over a gross profit of 30 percent, meeting our goal of at least 25 percent gross profit. Another way to measure profit is to aim to return three to four dollars for every one spent. In other words, we spent $15,000 on the Drake and increased the value based upon the appraiser's evaluation by $63,000. This makes for a yield of four dollars for every one dollar spent ($63,000 ÷ $15,000 = 4.20). This is an excellent return. Even a two- or three-dollar return on increased value would still represent an acceptable return.

Any way you look at it, the Drake was a success. Now it's time to use those same fundamentals on a new endeavor. We evaluate the Cypress with these parameters in mind. First we will examine the current income and expense.

The Cypress Apartments		
Annual Scheduled Gross Income		$26,400
- Less 5 Percent Vacancy Factor		- $1,320
Adjusted Gross Income		$25,080
Expenses		
Taxes	$2,636	
Insurance	$1,430	
Utilities	$3,120	
Maintenance (Est. 8 Percent)	$2,112	
Total Expenses	$9,298	
ESTIMATED NET INCOME		$15,782

Based upon an asking price of $220,000 and a net income of $15,782, we arrive at a capitalization rate of around 7 percent ($15,782 ÷ $220,000 = 0.07). Considering the entrepreneurial effort that will be required to maximize the property value, we feel that the capitalization should be higher, thereby making the price lower. We offer $189,000, which reflects a higher capitalization rate and a margin of safety to cover any unexpected expenses. At $189,000, the capitalization rate is 8 percent. We estimate that the cost to modernize the apartments will be the same as for the Drake, but with one additional apartment to upgrade. So total costs would be as follows: a purchase price of $189,000 plus $19,000 in renovation costs equals a total cost of $208,000.

After remodeling the apartments, will we be able to obtain our 25 percent gross profit? Let's break it down like we did before:

The Cypress Apartments		
Annual Scheduled Gross Income ($900 × 5 × 12)		$54,000
- Less 5 Percent Vacancy Factor		- $2,700
Adjusted Gross Income		$51,300
Expenses		
Taxes	$2,636	
Insurance	$1,430	
Utilities	$3,120	
Maintenance (Est. 8 Percent)	$4,320	
Total Expenses	$11,506	
NET INCOME		$39,794

At a capital value of 7 percent this new net income would represent a new value of approximately $568,000. We get that figure by dividing the net income (as estimated above) by the estimated capitalization rate for the neighborhood. For this area we determine that the capitalization rate is about 7 percent. We divide the net income of $39,794 by 0.07, which equals $568,486. This would certainly meet our profit goal and looks like it could be an exceptionally good deal.

When the economy is good and unemployment is low, vacancy factors tend to be low, thereby driving up apartment rents. In this case the owner probably has no idea of the true market rents for his apartments. This certainly contributes to our profit projections.

We realize no one is bidding on the property, so we stand firm on our offer of $189,000 with a $5,000 down payment. An important note about negotiations: You can sense when you are the only one interested. Both the broker and seller focus on your proposal with great interest. When they are somewhat aloof, you can get the feeling there is another offer on the table or that they are negotiating with another buyer.

In this case the broker lets us know he is negotiating only with us. We propose going with a contract of sale with the seller carrying his equity and collecting our monthly payments. We propose paying the seller upon completion of the improvements and refinancing the property with a new first trust deed, just as we did with the Drake. We ask the seller to carry most of the purchase price for five years. This will give us plenty of time to complete the improvements and establish rental history at the higher income levels.

The seller agrees to the purchase price of $189,000 but counters with the following:

- Down payment on the land contract will be $6,000
- Monthly payments will be $1,100
- Term of contract will be two years

We agree to the above terms but with a closing in forty-five days, as we need the time to collect the down payment and renovation expenses.

Since our fix-up costs are estimated at $19,000 and the down payment is $6,000, we look into refinancing the Drake to raise these funds and to create an operating reserve. After two and a half years, the income and expense on the Drake are as follows:

The Drake Apartments		
Annual Scheduled Gross Income		$38,400
- Less 5 Percent Vacancy Factor		- $1,920
Adjusted Scheduled Income		$36,480
Expenses		
Taxes	$1,560	
Insurance	$756	
Utilities	$1,020	
Maintenance (Est. 8 Percent)	$2,640	
Total Expenses	$5,976	
NET INCOME		$30,504

How to Refinance the Drake Apartments

The first step of a refinance is inquiring at the bank where we have our existing loan. Usually an existing relationship can net you better terms and some perks down the road. The bank indicates that, based on the net income of the property, it would be interested in making a larger loan. Our existing loan is only $93,000, so we expect that we can net our desired cash from this larger first loan.

We make arrangements for the bank's appraiser to meet us at the Drake so he can view the inside of each apartment. The appraiser makes notes on all of the completed improvements. He indicates that the tenants are new and are renting at the top end of the current market. The lender eventually commits to a new first trust deed in the amount of $204,000. This is based on an appraisal value of $300,000. Again, in this example, we are in a period of rising property values.

Since we will be netting the entire purchase price in this refinance, we decide to take this opportunity to replace the roof. The cost will be paid out of the proceeds from this transaction. As usual, we obtain three bids. We choose the roofer that we feel has the best combination of price and reputation, and we are confident that the company will do a good job. It is important that the roofer has been in business awhile because you can predict the likelihood that he will be in business in the future; you need a company that will be around to honor any warranty in the event that you have a problem with the new roof. For these reasons, often the roofer with the lowest bid will lose out. Be smart and use the information at your disposal; you will find contractors that you will use time and again, which can benefit everybody in the future.

At close of escrow on the new first trust deed, we pay off the existing loan of approximately $93,000, the $9,900 roof bill, and miscellaneous closing costs. We receive a closing check of $89,009, after all expenses are paid. It should be noted that the new payment is $1,095.12 including interest at 5 percent. These payments represent an amount that is less than the payment in the original land contract. After the new loan is put in place our new income/expense setup looks like this:

The Drake Apartments		
Monthly Scheduled Gross Income		$3,200
- Less 5 Percent Vacancy Factor		- $160
Adjusted Scheduled Income		$3,040
Expenses		
Taxes	$130	
Insurance	$63	
Utilities	$85	
Maintenance	$220	
Total Expenses	$498	
NET INCOME		$2,542
Loan Payment	$1,096	
IN-POCKET NET		$1,446

As per chapter 1, our overall objective in this endeavor is to generate income, so we decide, at least for the time being, to keep the Drake for this purpose. However, we will reserve some of the in-pocket net for future capital improvements at the Drake such as window replacements.

With our new loan proceeds deposited into our account, we are ready to close the deal on the five-unit property. It should be noted that the proceeds from refinancing are not taxable. That is because it is a loan and not a capital gain. Loans are paid back; capital gains are profit.

We hand over the $6,000 down payment to the seller and close our contract of sale on the Cypress Apartments. We begin making improvements to the two vacant units. The good thing about apartment buildings is that you can do improvements one unit at a time while you collect income on the other units that are rented. This helps your cash flow, which is particularly important on larger buildings with more units—but we will get to that soon enough.

After completing the improvements to the two-bedroom house and two-bedroom apartment, we find tenants to rent the units at higher rates. While we await turnover in the other units, we make exterior improvements: painting, changing the address signage, and landscaping.

Some of the other tenants become inspired to move because they want improved apartments like the ones our new tenants have received. It is difficult to modernize apartments while people are living in them, and it is almost impossible to raise the rents on existing tenants to what you want them to be after completion of the improvements. So it is best to wait for natural attrition.

Eventually we are able to make the appropriate improvements to the remaining apartments. After two years, our new income/expense setup is as follows:

The Cypress Apartments		
Annual Scheduled Gross Income		$61,200
- Less 5 Percent Vacancy Factor		- $3,060
Adjusted Scheduled Income		$58,140
Expenses		
Taxes	$2,636	
Insurance	$1,430	
Utilities	$4,510	
Maintenance (Est. 8 Percent)	$4,896	
Total Expenses	$13,472	
NET INCOME		$44,668
Less Land Contract Payments	$13,200	
NET IN-POCKET		$31,468

Since The Cypress is operating profitably after over two years of ownership, we decide to apply for a new first trust deed again. This will accomplish the following:

- Pay off the seller and the contract of sale
- Get the property deed in the name of our entity
- Reimburse our down payment and improvement costs
- Provide additional funds for investment

We apply at a local bank that is not the one we used for the Drake. This bank specializes in apartment-house loans and has been advertising heavily for loan applicants. Over the past two years we have established a history of higher rental income. This makes the bank feel more comfortable about the future of the building, which makes them open to doing business with us.

The bank's appraiser makes an appointment to see the Cypress. We make the usual arrangements for him to view the inside of the house and the four apartments.

As a result of his analysis, he estimates the market value of the Cypress to be $535,000. Based on this appraisal, the bank offers a new thirty-year first trust deed (mortgage) of $300,000. This includes interest at 6.5 percent. If we take the offer, our new monthly payment will be $1,896. This payment represents approximately 40 percent of the scheduled income on the Cypress. As first suggested in chapter 4, we maintain our rule of keeping mortgage payments under 45 to 50 percent of income.

We now factor this new loan payment into our projected income and expense setup:

The Cypress Apartments		
Monthly Scheduled Gross Income		$5,100
- Less 5 Percent Vacancy Factor		- $255
Adjusted Scheduled Gross Income		$4,845
Expenses		
Taxes	$220	
Insurance	$120	
Utilities	$376	
Maintenance	$408	
Total Expenses	$1,124	
NET INCOME		$3,721
New Loan Payment	$1,896	
NEW IN-POCKET NET		$1,825

The benefit of taking the new loan is that we will pocket approximately $100,000. In addition we will pay off the short-term land contract. The seller will get paid off, the broker will be paid out of the seller's proceeds, and the property will be deeded into our own entity. Also, with a long-term, low-interest amortizing first trust deed on the property, we will facilitate a possible sale sometime in the future.

We tell the bank that we will take the loan. Within several weeks we go to the title company and agree to pay one year of the property insurance in advance, the balance owing on the purchase price, and other miscellaneous closing costs. To our surprise, the bank has credited us with the appraisal fee of $1,400 that we paid for in advance.

After the recording of the new loan, we receive a check for $114,492 as net proceeds from the transaction.

Let's review our progress to date:

- Value of the Drake $340,000
  Outstanding Mortgage   - $204,000
       Equity $136,000

- Value of The Cypress $535,000
  Outstanding Mortgage   - $300,000
       Equity $235,000

Currently we have equity of $371,000 in our two properties. By refinancing upon completion of the improvements, we netted approximately $203,000 cash. We also created 40 percent equity in the Drake. In the Cypress we created equity of 44 percent. This is in line with our goal of 25 to 50 percent equity.

At this point we can continue to expand our acquisitions or simply keep these properties for income. We can just concentrate on paying off the mortgages and keeping the two properties in a retirement account.

But, for the time being, we concentrate on expanding our holdings. We have approximately $170,0000 to facilitate future investments. This breaks down as follows:

Proceeds from the Drake	$89,000
- Less Purchase and Improvements	-$25,000
Balance	$64,000
Net Refinance Proceeds from the Cypress	$114,000
New Balance	$178,000

However, before we proceed, we hire a reputable roofer to install a new roof on the home that is part of the Cypress for $7,800. It is at the end of its useful life.

Now, I will show a few more examples of how you might purchase additional properties, each one highlighting the same fundamentals that I have used here. Remember, we started all of this with a simple $15,000 in savings. If you feel like you understand the process of how this works, you can skip on to chapter 7. If you want to read further to see how to turn these two rental properties into a substantial income, please continue.

Still with me? Let us proceed.

Buying Your Third Property

On a popular Internet site dedicated to investment real estate, we notice an ad for the Commodore, a nine-unit apartment building located in an area of quiet single-family homes. We call the broker, and he sends the following income/expense details.

Commodore Apartments
Annual Property Operating Data

Nine-Unit Apartment Building

Asking Price	$395,000
Current 1st Loan	$281,000
Down Payment	$114,000
Price per unit:	$43,900
Total Monthly Rent:	$5,160/mo.

Operating Income:

Gross Rental Income	$61,920
Laundry Income	$780
Parking Income	
Vacancy & Credit Loss (4%)	-$2,477
Gross Operating Income	$60,223

Operating Expense:

Real Estate Taxes	1.25	$5,000	
Property Management	5%	$3,000	6.38% GRM
On-Site Management		$1,000	
Property Insurance		$2,000	9.22% Cap Rate
Repairs & Maint.		$2,000	
PG&E		$2,300	10% Cash on Cash
Water		$4,200	
Garbage		$2,300	Approx. Loan amort. yr. #1
Accounting & Legal		$500	$4,800
Advertising, License & Permits		$500	14.23% Total return yr. #1
Gardener/Landscape Maint.		$500	
Laundry Lease		-0-	
Miscellaneous & Reserves		$500	

Total Operating Expense 38%	$23,800	$2,644 per unit per year
Net Operating Income	$36,423	Current 1st Adjustable Loan
Annual Debt Service 1st Ln	-$24,996	fully indexed rate @ 7.17%
Cash Flow Before Income Taxes	$11,427	mo. pymt. @ $2,083 pymt.

We make no representation as to the accuracy of projections or as to the ability of any prospective buyer to achieve projected rent levels. We make no representations as to the accuracy of tax computations; they are estimates only. All prospective buyers are advised to consult with their CPA in determining actual tax effect from this investment.

Upon inspection of the property exterior, we notice that the front yard is mostly a weed patch. When we walk to the rear of the property, we see that the parking area is overcrowded with cars, most of which look like they do not run and have not been moved for some time. As we walk back to the front of the property, we notice that the laundry room door is propped open. We look inside and see that there is graffiti on the walls as well as some holes in the sheetrock.

We decide to call the broker back. Although the property seems to be neglected and in need of some attention, it does offer the potential that we are looking for. In addition, the asking price is in line with the value for buildings of this type in this neighborhood. We make an appointment with the broker to see the interiors of several units. Upon inspecting the interiors, we note that the kitchens, baths, and closet panel doors are all from the original construction. By the building's appearance, we can estimate that it was built in the early 1960s. We check to make sure the plumbing is copper and not galvanized pipe, as this will save us lots of money and headaches down the line. Galvanized piping tends to corrode and restrict water flow. Copper piping does not corrode and lasts a lifetime.

The average rents are in the $575 range. In doing some comparative rent analysis, we see that the rents could be significantly higher. To get substantially more income, however, we will need to do lots of upgrading similar to what we completed in our previous purchases.

At this time, the building is full at the lower rents. We estimate that we will need to spend about $5,000 per unit to modernize the interiors of the apartments. These can be done one at a time upon tenant turnover. With nine fully rented units, it will take longer to complete the improvements, and we estimate the process will take two years or more to complete.

Earlier, the broker told us that the building has been owned by a family for about ten years. The loan on the property is new, as the owners have recently refinanced the property. According to the broker there was an unexpected death in the family less than a year ago. The deceased was the person who took care of the property. Now the husband has taken over but does not have the time or interest to devote a lot of effort to it.

We tell the broker we will get back to him with a proposal. He insists that we put down at least 8 percent of the purchase price as down payment, as this would cover his commission and seller's closing costs. We tell him that the property needs to be upgraded and modernized at a cost of about $50,000, and he agrees that it does need work. At this point we figure that the fix-up costs, down payment, and closing costs will take up a substantial portion of our $170,0000 cash held for reserve and investment.

To counter the broker's suggestion and reserve as much cash as possible, we decide to offer a lease with an option to purchase the property on the following terms:

- Purchase price to be $360,000
- Security deposit and consideration for the option to be $13,000 cash
- Monthly payment to include the amount of the first trust deed loan plus a 7 percent return on the seller's equity (This will make for a monthly lease payment in the amount of $2,398. Of this amount the seller will keep $315, representing a return on his equity. The balance represents the existing, monthly mortgage payment.)
- Term of the lease/option to be five years

We communicate the offer to the broker, and we understand that it will take some time to educate the seller about this method of purchase. In the meantime we estimate what our income and expenses will be once the planned improvements are completed. We see that comparable remodeled two-bedroom apartments in the area are renting for $750.

The Commodore		
Monthly Scheduled Gross Income ($750 × 9)	$6,750	
- Less 5 Percent Vacancy Factor	- $338	
Adjusted Monthly Gross Scheduled Income	$6,412	
Expenses		
Taxes	$375	
Insurance	$167	
Utilities	$733	
Maintenance	$540	
Total Expenses	$1,815	
NET INCOME		$4,597
Less Lease Payment	$2,398	
NET IN-POCKET		$2,199

On an annual basis it would look as follows:

The Commodore		
Annual Scheduled Gross Income		$81,000
- Less 5 Percent Vacancy Factor		- $4,050
Adjusted Annual Gross Income		$76,950
Expenses		
Taxes	$4,500	
Insurance	$2,004	
Utilities	$8,796	
Maintenance (Est. 8 Percent)	$6,480	
Total Expenses	$21,780	
NET INCOME		$55,170
Less Lease Payments		$28,776
NET IN-POCKET		$26,394

We estimate the new capitalized value:

- At a gross rent multiplier of seven, it would be $567,000.
- At a capitalization rate of 9 percent, it would be about $600,000.

If we consider our total purchase price of $410,000 (our improvement expenses of $50,000 plus a purchase price of $360,000), our gross profit would be as follows:

New Value	$580,000 (blend of above)
Cost	$410,000
Margin	$170,000

We calculate our gross profit to be 29 percent ($170,000 ÷ $580,000 = 0.29). This falls within our goal of 25 to 50 percent gross profits. Also if we spend $50,000 in remodeling and get back approximately $170,000, we will have achieved our profit ratio of three to one. In other words, we'll be getting back three dollars for every one dollar spent on improvements. You make money in real estate when you buy; you realize it when you sell or refinance.

We wait patiently to get the seller's response. After ten days have passed we finally hear that the seller accepts our lease-option proposal with the following counter:

- Real estate commission to be paid outside of the transaction but deducted from the purchase price
- Terms of lease-option to be three years—not five, as we proposed

We counter the term to be four years but to no avail. The seller is firm on this point. In negotiating the broker's commission, we agree to the following installments:

- $5,000 due at signing
- Annual installments thereafter of $4,333 until paid

A lease-option agreement is drafted incorporating all of the above terms. All parties sign the agreement. Also we draft a memorandum of option to be recorded against the property at the county recorder's office. This protects our interest by putting a notation on the title. As with our other acquisitions, we collect the first month's rent and use it as an initial installment for the broker's fee.

Since there are no vacancies in the apartments, we begin our upgrade/ remodel by cleaning up the exterior of the property. We arrange to have the nonoperating cars removed from the premises. We make arrangements to install a new lawn and automatic sprinkler system where the weed patch was in the front of the property. Our painter does the necessary prep work to repaint the wood trim on the exterior of the property. These are simple steps to begin what will be a major transformation.

While the above work is being done, one tenant gives notice that he intends to move. We line up labor and materials to completely remodel the apartment. This remodel will be similar to all the other rehabs that were done in both the fourplex and the five-unit properties described earlier in this chapter, so there really are not any surprises. With this step, we have begun the task of modernizing each of the two-bedroom apartments.

As vacancies come up, we completely modernize each apartment. We have good luck in renting the newly renovated apartments at the higher rents, and we continue this process as our tenants move out. The new rents are in line with what we estimated before buying the property. Our new rent for each vacancy is $750, an additional $200 (more than a 35 percent increase from the old rents). Our improvements are paying off; in two and a half years, we have completed the modernization of the interior of all nine units.

Our income and expense data now looks as follows:

The Commodore		
Annual Scheduled Gross Income		$79,460
- Less 5 Percent Vacancy Factor		- $3,973
Adjusted Annual Gross Income		$75,487
Expenses		
Taxes	$5,450	
Insurance	$2,570	
Utilities	$10,431	
Maintenance (Est. 8 Percent)	$7,480	
Total Expenses	$25,931	
NET INCOME		$49,556
Less Lease Payments	$28,776	
NET IN-POCKET		$20,780

At this time we plan to obtain a new first trust deed to both pay off the seller's equity and put the deed into our entity. Our method of holding property will be discussed in a later chapter, so for right now, we will repeat our earlier processes. Again we apply at a local bank that specializes in apartment loans. In this case we go back to the same bank we used for the Drake. Our credit is well established there, after six years of business transactions. Since the property is the primary security for any loan you get, the lender is normally interested mainly in the value of the property. This means the appraisal and analysis of the property's income is of utmost importance.

We show the lender our tax returns to establish the income history of the property. Remember, two years' worth of seasoning should be enough for most lenders. Upon the banker's satisfaction, she orders an appraisal. Some lenders do not have their own appraisal departments, so they will ask you to order and pay for an appraisal from their recommended list of reputable appraisers. This was the case in the refinancing of the five-unit apartment building. However, the lender is so interested in getting new loans that it agrees to reimburse our appraisal. Beware that income property appraisals are much more expensive than single-family home estimates.

We arrange to meet the appraiser at the property. We emphasize the improvements that have been completed. We also provide him with an up-to-date rent roll and list of expenses as well as signed copies of each rental agreement.

After his analysis, the appraiser determines that the apartments have a value of $550,000. This is acceptable to us and is in line with our original estimation of upgraded value.

During the time that the loan is being processed, we open escrow and determine what has to be paid so that we can close on the new loan.

We determine the following: The principal balance of the existing first trust deed is $259,410. The balance when we began the lease option was $279,358. Our lease payments included principal paydown on the loan. Thus we have reduced the amount owing on the first mortgage by $19,948. We will receive credit in escrow for this amount. Other costs that will need to be paid in escrow include the following:

Loan Origination Fee	$2,400
Insurance Payment Advance	$1,213
Title Insurance	$1,886
City Transfer Tax	$4,800
Escrow Fee	$614
Total	$10,913

The broker's fees have already been paid, as we made installments to him during the lease. At this time the balance owed to the seller is $41,691. So we conclude that whatever loan amount we are offered, it must be enough to pay off the current first, all closing costs, and monies owed to the seller—approximately $312,014 in all.

The loan officer calls us to say that the loan will be in the amount of $320,000. The monthly payment will be $1,919.00 including interest at a starting rate of 6 percent. Since this is lower than our past lease payments, the annual net income will increase by about $5,500. This represents a loan to value (LTV) of about 60 percent. We think it over for a few days and then tell her we will go ahead with it. At close of escrow we receive a check for approximately $7,986.

Keep in mind that various lenders have different ground rules. Some lenders will base a loan on appraised value; some will only lend on a percentage of the option price. It is helpful if you document all of your improvement costs.

We spent almost $50,000 for improvements over the past two and a half years. When added to the cost of $360,000, this amounts to a total of $410,000 spent. We paid down the loan by almost $20,000 through the lease payments, which came from the income on the property. We will consider the $20,000 principal paydown as a bonus and forced savings.

So if we consider that the net cost of the property is $390,000 and our current value is $550,000, we have created a 29 percent gross profit. Also, we met our goal when you consider that we received over three dollars back for every dollar spent on upgrading. That is a $160,000 gain in value beyond the purchase price and in consideration of $50,000 spent on improvements.

Our projected annual net income on our three properties is estimated to be as follows:

The Drake	$12,000
The Cypress	$21,000
The Commodore	$25,000
Total	$58,000

Again, this is net income (profit). Remember, we started with $15,000 in savings, and we are now making almost $60,000 annually in *profit*. With this level of success, we decide to shop for our fourth property.

Buying Your Fourth Property
We raise our sights a little and begin to search for a property with at least sixteen units. At this level and above, there is normally a resident manager

living on the premises. This will make the job of management much easier for us. We search various broker's Internet listings and newspaper ads. Most of these sellers want all cash for their properties. Needless to say, with our methods of financing it would be difficult to make an all-cash deal. We are looking for motivated sellers; in many cases, they are tired of the management chores. It is helpful if the seller has owned the property a long time; for our purposes, the longer, the better. I would say ten years should be the minimum. The only exception might be when the owners of the property picked up the building for an extraordinarily low price, for example, if they bought it from a foreclosing lender, as was the case with our original fourplex seller.

These sellers are not usually trying to squeeze every dime from the property. Also the mortgages and taxes on these properties are likely to be low. Often these sellers are open to receiving monthly payments over time.

During our search, we find an advertised sixteen-unit property called the Rosewood Apartments. We put in a call to the broker, who informs us that the seller wants to get cashed out on this property. *Cashed out* means the seller does not want to carry any financing to help the buyer purchase the property. We inspect the property and find the condition to be similar to what the Commodore was before we upgraded it. We know from experience that it is unlikely that the seller will get an all-cash offer, considering the price he is asking and the condition of the building. Sellers can get higher prices for their properties when they offer terms. This was the situation on our previous buys. We paid a little more than the properties would warrant for quick all-cash closings. With income property, prices are normally discounted for all-cash deals. Only properties in outstanding locations might mitigate this.

We tell the broker to keep in touch, especially in the event that the property does not sell. Meanwhile we continue to look for income properties in this size range. We make additional inquiries and a few offers, but nothing materializes.

Finally, several months after the initial contact, the broker of the Rosewood Apartments calls to say his seller will entertain an offer from us. We begin our analysis of this new property by studying the following property operating data provided to us by the salesman:

Rosewood Apartments
Sixteen Apartment Units

This three-story building of 9,825 square feet is located on an 8,150-square-foot lot and consists of ten one-bedroom, one-bath units and six studio units. Each unit is separately metered for electricity and gas, tenant paid. Each unit also has a separate hot water heater, the gas paid by tenant. Owner pays for water and garbage. The building is a wood frame/stucco exterior with parking underneath for ten cars. The roof is tar and gravel. The property is fenced and gated. There is some deferred maintenance at present. Management available.

There is currently an older loan on the property. Buyer will want to obtain new financing. Seller would like a cash-out sale. Make offer subject to inspection. Do not disturb tenants.

The Rosewood Apartments
Projected Annual Property Operating Data

16-Unit Apartment Building

Asking Price	$525,000
Current 1st Loan	$367,500
Down Payment	$157,500
Price per unit:	$33,000
Total Monthly Rent:	$7,180/mo.

Operating Income:

Gross Rental Income	$81,852
Laundry Income	$800
Parking Income	
Vacancy & Credit Loss (4%)	-$4,308
Gross Operating Income	$76,744

Operating Expense:

Real Estate Taxes	1.25%	$6,600	
Property Management	5%	$4,000	6.4% GRM
On-Site Management		$1,000	
Property Insurance		$2,700	9.29% Cap Rate
Repairs & Maint.		$4,000	
PG&E		$1,000	10.92% Cash on Cash
Water		$4,100	
Garbage		$2,550	Approx. Loan amort. yr. #1
Accounting & Legal		$500	$3,225
Advertising, License & Permits		$500	12.97% Total return yr. #1
Gardener/Landscape Maint.		$500	
Laundry Lease		-0-	
Miscellaneous & Reserves		$500	

Total Operating Expense 38%	$27,950	$2,644 per unit per year
Net Operating Income	$48,794	Current 1st Adjustable Loan
Annual Debt Service 1st Ln	-$31,594	fully indexed rate @ 7.17%
Cash Flow Before Income Taxes	$17,200	mo. pymt. @ $2,083 pymt.

We make no representation as to the accuracy of projections or as to the ability of any prospective buyer to achieve projected rent levels. We make no representations as to the accuracy of tax computations; they are estimates only. All prospective buyers are advised to consult with their CPA in determining actual tax effect from this investment.

We can see that the average monthly rent per unit is about $425. Based on our research of this neighborhood, we realize this is about 25 percent under market. Rents have risen substantially in the past two years. As usual, in order to obtain increased rents, the building needs to be significantly upgraded.

Upon inspection of the interiors, we confirm that the defects are curable. The apartments need remodeled baths and kitchens. The exterior of the building needs new paint. The front of the building needs a new lawn and automatic sprinkler system. In fact, landscaping in the front of the property is so rundown that the tenants have begun to park their cars on it. We determine that the apartments need the same items replaced as in our other apartments that we have rehabilitated, which will help with our cost calculations.

After we complete the remodeling we estimate that the one-bedrooms can be rented for $700 and the studios for $500. This would give us a new annual gross scheduled income of $120,000—approximately a 50 percent increase in income. Since the expenses would not change that much, we can assume we have an opportunity to increase the capitalized value of the building by 50 percent. This is exactly what we are looking for. We do realize the remodeling will need to be done one apartment at a time and will be done on tenant turnover. The cost will be similar to our other upgraded apartments, about $5,000 per unit.

Later we discover that the apartments were built in 1951. We assume that, since the building is of this vintage, the plumbing is more than likely galvanized piping and at least some of it will need to be replaced. We estimate this cost and factor it into our budget.

In our negotiations with the realtor we emphasize all that we will need to do to make it a viable property. As in the negotiations of our previous properties, we want to keep the mortgage, or lease payment, at 45 percent of our current income or less. When the expenses are added to the monthly payment this will ensure that we maintain a margin of safety.

We tell the broker we would like to do a lease option similar to what we arranged for our previous property. For some reason, the sellers are more willing to accept a smaller down payment to accommodate a lease option.

Some sellers view it as a security deposit, and since they are not conveying title, they are sometimes more comfortable with it.

The realtor emphasizes that if we expect the seller to give us the terms we want, we will need to come in close to the asking price. Again, since the property has been on the market for about four months, we realize we are probably the only buyers in sight, at least for the time being.

Our initial offer is for an option price of $475,000 with $10,000 down as security deposit and consideration for the option to purchase. We ask for a five-year term. After further negotiations over the next two weeks, we finally agree to the following:

- Purchase price to be $495,000
- Option consideration of $10,000
- Term to be two years with seller's equity of $269,550 to be paid at that time
- Underlying loan of $210,450 and monthly payments of $1,428 to be included in lease payment of $3,000 per month
- Broker's fee to be paid outside of escrow (The purchase price is to be reduced by this amount.)
- Property to be purchased as is

The existing gross monthly income is $6,821. This fits within our objective of maintaining mortgage payments that are within the parameters of the property's income.

Next we work out a deal with the broker to pay the $15,000 fee as follows: $2,500 will be paid now, and $500 will be paid per month until we exercise the option to purchase. Any balance still owing will be paid at close of escrow. Everyone signs the deal. We pay the required amounts to the seller and broker, and then we get to work on our fourth acquisition.

Over the next two years we make a number of improvements:

- New three-color exterior paint job
- New mailboxes
- New landscaping
- New ceramic tile kitchen floors
- New plumbing fixtures

- New bathroom vanities and sinks
- Fresh paint in the apartments that have turned over
- New window coverings in apartments
- New kitchen countertops and new stainless steel sinks
- New kitchen sink cabinet bases
- New kitchen cabinets to replace original steel cabinets
- New carpeting

By the end of twenty-four months we have completed twelve of the sixteen apartments. The rental income has been increased to our projected levels. This is how our new income and expense data looks:

The Rosewood Apartments		
Annual Scheduled Gross Income		$113,820
- Less 5 Percent Vacancy Factor		- $5,691
Adjusted Annual Gross Income		$108,129
Expenses		
Taxes	$8,450	
Insurance	$3,200	
Utilities	$7,650	
Maintenance	$9,106	
Total Expenses	$28,406	
NET INCOME		$79,723
Less Lease Payments	$36,000	
IN-POCKET NET INCOME		$43,723

Improvements and upgrading of the apartments over the past two years increased the gross scheduled income from approximately $81,000 to $113,000—an increase of 40 percent!

Again the time has come to place a new long-term first trust deed on the property. It pays to watch interest rates and how they fluctuate so you can refinance at a time that will benefit you. If ever the rates drop below normal market value, it would be a good time to seek a refi (refinancing) to obtain a new long-term first on the property. This would also be a good opportunity to pay off the seller's equity. Once the seller is paid off, we can place the property in the name of our own entity. If interest rates are rising and money is tight, we could always negotiate with the seller to extend his loan. We could offer to pay a little more interest to entice him to extend. Since we have developed a good net income, this increased interest would be supported by the property. It is good to have options.

We apply at a local bank that has been advertising apartment house loans. The bank officer reviews the above income and expense data. Since it appears that the property's income would support our requested loan, she orders an appraisal of the apartments. Based on our new gross and net income from the property she determines the new value to be $855,000.

Taking this new value into consideration, we determine our gross profit to be as follows:

Purchase Price	$495,000
Improvement Costs	$70,000
Total Cost	$565,000
New Value	$855,000
Purchase & Improvement Costs	$565,000
Gross Profit and Equity	$290,000

So we crunch the numbers and come up with 34 percent ($290,000 ÷ $855,000 = 0.34). This is excellent news.

This time the realized profit is four times the amount of the upgrading expenses. In other words, we improved the value by four dollars for every dollar spent on improvements. This ratio is better than what we achieved on our other properties. Often a larger property yields a higher return.

In a couple of weeks the loan officer offers us a loan of $560,000, a 65 percent loan-to-value ratio based on the appraisal. She also informs us that the monthly payments will be $2,923.20 including interest of 4.75 percent. Before we commit, we analyze how the loan will be disbursed.

Our largest expense is paying off the option purchase price. The sum of $269,500, minus one half of the city transfer tax, goes to the seller. This new amount is $265,300. The existing first trust deed in the amount of $188,110 will also be paid off from the proceeds, so $453,410 ($265,300 + $188,110) must come out of the new first loan right off the top. When we started the lease payments, the existing amount owing on the underlying loan was approximately $210,000. Portions of our lease payments have paid the loan down by $21,890. From the new proceeds we must pay off the balance of the realtor's commission of $7,500 as well as our half of the city transfer tax and title and escrow charges. The balance due to us at close of escrow amounts to $81,630.

So the benefits of the loan are as follows:

- We reimburse ourselves the upgrading and improvement costs.
- We pay off the seller's interest in the property.
- We put the deed in our own entity.
- We do all of the above and our net, in-pocket income stays as is. This is because the new loan payment is nearly the same as the lease payments we have been making.

Without any doubts we accept the loan and proceed to close escrow.

Our annual net income from the four properties is approaching $100,000! Before we pat ourselves on the back, though, there is still work to be done to maximize those profits. So now we look again to a refinance.

How to Refinance the Commodore Apartments

As we discussed earlier, the cash you obtain by refinancing will not be taxable when you get the additional funds; this is because loan funds have to be paid back. Many investors have made fortunes by refinancing instead of selling desirable properties in order to keep expanding.

It has been several years since we obtained our new loans equal to our out-of-pocket purchase and improvement costs. During this time we have continued to improve the operations of the properties. As a result, the income has improved substantially.

It is decided that we will refinance our holdings if:

- our equity is at least 50 percent of the property's current value; and
- we can obtain a larger loan at an interest rate that will not substantially change our existing monthly payments of principal and interest.

The first property considered is the Commodore Apartments. We will consider the income and expenses and come up with an estimation of value.

Commodore Apartments		
Annual Scheduled Gross Income		$129,600
- Less 5 Percent Vacancy Factor		- $6,480
Adjusted Annual Gross Income		$123,120
Expenses		
Taxes	$6,790	
Insurance	$3,089	
Utilities	$10,802	
Maintenance	$10,368	
Total Expense	$31,049	
NET INCOME		$92,071

Using a gross rent multiplier of 7.75 gives us a value of $1,000,000 (7.75 × $129,600 = $1,000,000). Using a capitalization rate of 8.5 percent gives us a value of approximately $1,000,000. That is net income of $92,071 divided by 0.0850, which equals $1,083,188 (we round down to $1,000,000 to be conservative). Both the gross rent multiplier and capitalization factors are typical for the neighborhood.

This establishes our first requirement to have at least 50 percent equity. If we owe approximately $303,066 on our existing first trust deed (it was originally $320,000) and our estimate of current value is $1,000,000, this leaves about $696,000 as equity (calculated by subtracting $303,066 from $1,000,000). This makes for an equity position of 70 percent.

If we calculate that the lender will make a 60 percent loan on a refinance, we can estimate a loan offer between $500,000 to $600,000, depending on the actual result of the appraisal. Normally on a purchase and with cash down payment, the lender would lend between 70 and 75 percent. A refinance is usually in the 60 to 65 percent range.

The lender that we intend to use has quoted us a beginning interest rate of 4.75 percent. In checking an amortization chart, we determine that the monthly payment on a $550,000 loan amortized over thirty years at this rate would be $2,769.06. This amount would easily be supported by the net income from the property but is higher than our existing payment.

We decide to apply for the refinance. The bank makes an offer of $575,000 for a new mortgage. This represents an almost 60 percent loan-to-value ratio. The estimated title and escrow charges will be approximately $2,433. After considering this, we decide to accept the new loan.

At the close of escrow we pick up a check for $259,985. We spend an additional $5,943 dollars on a new 100-gallon water heater for the building and still have enough left over in our annual operating budget for any additional upgrades.

After some time, you should have some property clear of loans to provide a margin of safety. When you own a number of properties on which loans are liquidating through regular payments from income, you are in a much better position to finance emergencies or sudden opportunities if you are able to keep one property clear. It is much more advantageous to arrange some heavier mortgages to help clear others rather than to have all loans partially paid down. With some of the proceeds of our refinancing, we pay down principal on our home loan.

Our net income is well into six figures now! Again, if you feel comfortable with the example, you can skip ahead to chapter 7, but I have one more example I'd like to share with you—buying the fifth property.

Buying Your Fifth Property

We've spent the last few years managing our properties, maximizing our returns, and refinancing when it was appropriate. One day we get a phone call from a broker we know. The broker sends us the following property operating statement. The economy is in recession now, and competition to buy property is limited. Still our broker friend tells us the seller of this property wants all cash at the close of escrow. We regretfully tell him that we would only be interested in the event that she is not able to find an all-cash buyer.

In the meantime we study the income and expense statement that the broker sent us.

PROPERTY ANALYSIS
PARK TERRACE APARTMENTS
LISTING PRICE: $1,800,000

	# of Units	Type of Unit	SQFT	Ave. Curr. Rent
	14	1/1.0	662	$ 820
	6	2/1.0	851	$ 1,028
Total	20		14,374	$17,645
Annual Rental Income				$211,740
Less: Vacancy				($10,587)
Laundry				$3,600
Effective Income				$204,753
EXPENSES				
Property Taxes				$24,084
Special Assessments				$5,094
Insurance				$6,000
Water and Sewer				$16,500
Garbage				$5,880

Electricity and Gas	$10,800
Cleaning and Maintenance	$10,000
Business Tax	$3,003
Capital Reserves	$4,000
Rent Board Fees	$300
Management	$10,500
TOTAL EXPENSES	$96,161
EXPENSES / SQ FT	$6.69
EXPENSES/UNIT	$4,808
EXPENSE/GI	44.66%
Net Operating Income	$108,592
Less: Debt Service	$70,200
Projected Net Cash Flow	$38,392
Cash on Cash Return	5.33%
Price per Unit	$125.23
GIM	8.4%
CAP	6.03%

We note that the same family has owned this twenty-unit building for over twenty years. This is always a good sign. (The Commodore was owned by the same seller for over ten years, and the Rosewood was owned by the same owner for over eighteen years.)

It has been my experience that many income properties turn over every three or four years. It is a consistent pattern on some properties. I am very suspicious of these situations, because often it is because there is some incurable defect in the property or neighborhood—and you can be sure that neither the seller nor the broker will not tell you what it may be. This should always be a red flag on any potential deal.

So far our experience has been good in dealing with long-term owners. With long-term ownership you are least likely to encounter an overfinanced property, property taxes are likely to be low, and there will be an established history of income and expense. Finally, you can bet that the property is probably a good income producer. Why else would the seller have had it so long?

Unit mix on the Park Terrace property is fourteen one-bedroom units and six two-bedroom units. The units are separately metered for gas and electricity. Each apartment has forced-air heating. This is very unusual, as most apartments in the area simply have single wall heaters. Each apartment also has a parking space in the secured garage. Most working tenants want this feature, and it makes for a great selling point for new tenants.

The building is located in a good neighborhood of the city, but the units would not be considered luxury apartments. The property was built in 1958 and more than likely has copper plumbing, which is a bonus. The neighborhood in which the building is located has very well maintained single-family homes, and the street is lined with trees.

We realize this would be a desirable holding. Also the property lends itself to improvements and upgrading. It is in need of exterior paint in modern colors. We can also assume that the interiors probably need upgrading and modernization as well. But this will be determined if our offer gets accepted in the event that the seller will entertain less than an all-cash offer.

We determine that, if the seller decides to carry the financing, there will probably be competition to buy the property. When terms are offered, this simply opens the property up to more buyers, although one thing in our favor is that the economy is slow.

In the few years leading up to the recession, it was impossible to make a reasonable deal on income property. Investors were selling their smaller properties and trading up to larger income properties for which they paid extremely inflated prices. Most of these properties were reassessed for property taxes that put undue pressure on the expense side. Many properties went into foreclosure because they were overfinanced and overtaxed. Many investors lost their hard-earned down payments. When the real estate market heats up to frothy levels, it often pays to stay out of it, be patient, and wait for more rational times. Always be extremely cautious in making sure that you can handle the financing and property expenses from existing income, and always be sure to include a margin of safety.

We continue to further analyze the existing income and expense of the Park Terrace Apartments. The broker tells us that the actual property taxes are approximately $12,136 per year. We will use this figure for our income and expense sheet, because, as with the lease option, the property will not be reassessed immediately.

In the course of our analysis, we note that the water bill is double what it should be for a building of this size. We agree to examine this further when we inspect the interiors of the apartments. Our previous experiences with our other buildings tell us that, if the toilets are changed to low-flow models, the water bill can be reduced by up to one-half. (Some municipal water utilities will even reimburse you for your costs in doing this.)

Cleaning, maintenance, and management expenses at first glance look to be high in proportion to the building's income. The broker tells us the manager lives next door and has been doing the job for thirty years. If a new owner takes over, however, the building manager plans to retire. This is a good thing because, more than likely, our management style will be different from what he has been doing for so long. Our plans for improvements, upgrading, and increasing the rental income may seem unrealistic to him. We will think of this as a changing of the guard.

As a result of this, we lower estimates for management and cleaning expenses and actually include a revised figure in our maintenance budget that includes management. We also factor in 7 percent more rental income, as some rents can be raised immediately. Our revised estimates of income and expense are below.

The Park Terrace 20-Unit Apartment	
Annual Scheduled Gross Income	$226,562
- Less 5 Percent Vacancy Factor	- $11,328
Adjusted Annual Gross Income	$215,234
Laundry Income	$3,600
Total Gross Income	$218,834

Expenses	
Taxes	$12,136
Insurance	$6,000
Utilities	$24,930
Maintenance	$18,124
Total Expenses	$61,190
ANNUAL INCOME	$157,644

The broker tells us that the monthly payment on the adjustable rate first trust deed is $6,165.23. The annual payment at this amount would be $73,982.76, which is easily covered by the net income as figured above. The principal balance of the loan is $1,092,651 with an annual interest rate of 4.04 percent. The asking price is $1,800,000. At this asking price the seller's equity would be as follows:

Asking Price	$1,800,000
Existing Loan Balance	- $1,092,651
Current Equity	$707,349

We realize that in order to make this deal happen we will need to provide the seller with a reasonable return on her equity. If we make a down payment of $100,000 representing 6 percent, the balance of the purchase price being carried back by the seller would be about $600,000. In order to provide the seller with a 5 percent return, our monthly payment would be $2,500. If we add the first trust deed payment to this, our total monthly payment will be $8,665. We know from our analysis that the monthly net income is $13,137 ($157,644 ÷ 12 = $13,137). This would make for a monthly cash flow of $4,472 and annual cash flow of $53,664. This represents over 50 percent return on our down payment. But don't forget we will have some upgrading and improvement costs on apartment turnovers. We also realize the exterior of the building will need to be painted.

In proposing our plan to the broker, he tells us that in order for the seller to accept these terms we will need to raise our offer to a figure that is closer to the asking price. He also says that another buyer is offering to buy on terms similar to ours. Later he also explains that the motivation of the seller is to be relieved of management chores and receive a monthly income for her equity. We think we are on the way to making a reasonable deal. The cash flow and opportunity to upgrade the building while increasing the rental income are our prime motivations.

We assist the broker in writing up a lease option with the above stated terms, an option consideration of $100,000, and monthly payments that include paying the first mortgage and providing the seller with payments of $2,500 a month. The purchase price is to be $1,780,000. Since we are in the midst of an economic slowdown, we ask for a five-year term. We also make it a point to put in the contract that the buyer is to receive credit for all principal paydowns on the first mortgage during the term of the lease. The total sum of these principal paydowns will be credited against the purchase price when we exercise our option to buy.

After a few days the broker tells us that the seller is considering our offer but must discuss it with her accountant. After another week passes, the broker calls to tell us that the seller has accepted our offer. Since our offer is contingent upon our inspection, we make arrangements to get into the interiors of all of the apartments. We note that four of the units are vacant. Almost all of the units are original from when the building was erected in 1958.

We make notes on the work to be done:

Modernize and Remodel:

Kitchens

- Replace tiles with new laminate countertops
- Replace old cast iron sinks with stainless steel
- Replace worn linoleum flooring with ceramic tile

Baths

- Replace worn shower walls with new three-wall tub kits
- Replace old sink basins with up-to-date vanities and new sinks
- Replace toilets with low-flow toilets
- Replace worn linoleum floors

Upon completion of our inspection, we remove this contingency and ask the seller to reduce the purchase price to cover the cost of the above deficiencies. The seller refuses to do so. We decide to go ahead with the deal anyway. However, we do make it part of the contract that the owner must not rent the vacant units. This will enable us to renovate them to our satisfaction before they are occupied. I have almost never gotten credits for modernizing. For repairs, however, there is a good chance of purchase-price reductions.

Several weeks later, the escrow is closed, and the lease-option agreement is signed. Our $100,000 option consideration and security deposit is partially offset by the first month's rent and existing security deposits held by the seller on behalf of the tenants. This is possible because we arrange for lease payments to be paid in arrears. This is the same way normal interest and principal are paid on almost all mortgages. Our initial payment is not due until the first of the following month.

We receive a credit for rents paid in advance and deposits in escrow for $22,646. Prorated rents and credit for security deposits can reduce the amount of cash we need to close the deal.

We begin to upgrade the vacant units immediately, and upon completion, rent them at increased rents.

During our first six months we make numerous repairs to fix plumbing leaks throughout the property. We also arrange to replace all twenty toilets with up-to-date, low-flow models. As expected, all of the above contribute to reducing our water consumption. Almost all of these repairs are paid for from the net income from the property, so we accrue no out-of-pocket costs. We contact our local water utility company to provide receipts for the cost of the new low-flow toilets, and they arrange to credit our water bill until we are fully reimbursed.

As turnover occurs at the apartments, we modernize each one before they are rented again, as we have done with the units in each of our other properties. We also begin our exterior paint project. Most of the above is completed during the first six months of running the property. Rents are gradually increased as we go.

So during the first six months we have accomplished most of what we planned to do. At the end of the following year we are satisfied that the property has provided a $54,000 in-pocket net income. As a result we are satisfied with the income from the property. We continue to upgrade the apartments from the maintenance and repair budget that we designated for the building.

The seller is happy with the steady monthly income she receives on her equity, and we are excited that we are slowly upgrading the property, which will increase the net income. We all win.

How to Refinance the Rosewood Apartments

When you own larger, more desirable apartment buildings, like the Rosewood Apartments, our fourth property, it usually pays to save on turnover charges by holding the property and refinancing it in order to obtain funds to purchase other properties.

As with the Commodore, we will consider refinancing the Rosewood Apartments if our equity is at least 50 percent. Our second consideration is that we would like to obtain an advantageous interest rate and monthly payment. We realize that we are in a recession, which usually creates an environment of low rates. It may be possible to get a rate that is a little lower than what we are currently paying.

It has been several years since we completed our improvements and obtained our new loan to complete our purchase. In the interim, we have continued to upgrade the property and increase the income from rents. Now we will consider the up-to-date income and expenses and come up with an estimation of value.

The Rosewood **16-Unit Apartment**	
Annual Scheduled Gross Income	$145,931
- Less 5 Percent Vacancy Factor	- $7,296
Adjusted Gross Income	$138,635
Expenses	
Taxes	$12,165
Insurance	$5,120
Utilities	$10,507
Maintenance	$11,674
Total Expenses	$39,466
NET INCOME	$99,169

Using a gross rent multiplier of 7.75 gives us a value of $1,131,000. Using a capitalization rate of 8.5 percent gives us a value of $1,167,000. That is net income of $99,169 divided by 0.0850 = $1,167,000. For our purposes we round down to $1,100,000, again being conservative. Both the gross rent multiplier and capitalization factors are typical for the neighborhood; these values are more than likely what an appraiser would come up with.

We owe a balance on our first trust deed of $516,170. The original balance was $560,000, but we have paid it down by $43,830 from the income from the property. We calculate our equity as follows:

Estimate Value	$1,100,000
First Loan Balance	- $516,170
Current Equity	$583,830

$583,830 ÷ $1,100,000 = 0.53 (i.e., 53 percent)

We have satisfied our first requirement that we have at least 50 percent equity in the property. Based on the above information, we estimate that we will get a loan of between $700,000 and $800,000.

We apply at our local lender, and they start the refinancing process. We are surprised to learn that the appraiser has valued the property at

$1,200,000. The lender offers a loan of $824,000, which represents a loan to value of 69 percent. The interest rate will be 5.5 percent adjustable, making for a monthly payment of $4,680. Our new cash flow from the building is laid out below.

Annual Net Income	$99,169
Annual Loan Payments	- $56,160
In-Pocket Cash Flow	$43,009

Because the interest rate is reasonable and the payments still allow for a good in-pocket net, we go ahead with the loan. We feel that this has sufficiently met our second objective of requiring payments that the property can easily support. At close of escrow, after paying off our existing first trust deed and title expenses of $3,103, we are left with a check for $295,129.

It is a good idea to always borrow more, rather than less, than you need. Many investors borrow increasing amounts when the money is not actually needed, so that they can establish a reputation for repaying larger loans as promised. It is sound business to borrow more rather than less than needed. This gives you a reserve cushion and enables you to avoid additional closing costs and fees if you ever need to refinance again.

The management of the property itself offers additional reasons for why borrowing more than you need is a good idea. You might initiate a remodeling project that would necessitate emptying out tenants for a temporary period, thus limiting your income for a period of time. If you borrow exactly what you estimate that you will need and run into extra costs, you can (and will) be caught short. If your costs run as estimated and you don't refill your apartments as soon as expected, your rental income may not be enough in the short term to make the loan payments as scheduled. Try to borrow more than you expect you will need in order to provide yourself with a reserve fund.

There is also a downside to constant refinancing or being caught without adequate cash reserves for the "little things" that can come up. You can damage your credit and your peace of mind if you borrow less than you need and then fall behind on your payments and/or your property taxes. Keep this in mind: the more you borrow when you don't need the money, the more your credit ceiling will be raised when financing gets tight.

In this chapter I demonstrated how someone could start with a very small amount of capital and grow it to an important sum. You can build up a substantial net income from your property and achieve financial independence. At the same time you can grow rich by increasing your net worth with each property you acquire and improve.

Chapter Recap

This chapter identified core fundamentals that will help you build a real estate portfolio without subjecting yourself to undue risk.

- It is important to find motivated sellers. You *can* afford to pick and choose.
- Limit risk by making only small down payments.
- Mortgage payments and property expenses must fall within parameters that provide a margin of safety. Stick to these parameters.
- Modernize and update properties to attract desirable tenants that can afford increased rents; but be certain that the new rents never exceed the limits for the particular neighborhood.
- Substantial increases in the property values provide refinancing opportunities that facilitated further expansion and additional properties, each with limited risk and potential to increase the capital value.

-7-

How to Manage Your Apartments

Resolve never to quit, never to give up, no matter what the situation.

—Jack Nicklaus, golfer

Property management is people management. After you have renovated an apartment according to the suggestions in chapter 5 and obtained a desirable tenant, you must strive to keep that tenant happy and your turnover low. Whenever someone moves out, you must spend time and money for cleaning, painting, and carpeting for the next tenant. It also takes time and money to find an acceptable tenant. For you as the owner, high turnover puts a serious dent in your money machine. You absolutely must strive to keep your residents satisfied and keep turnover low. I call it the number-one rule to remember in this chapter—and for good reason.

Your apartments are a business. But to the tenants who pay you rent, an apartment is a home, a place to be comfortable, and maybe a place to raise a family. They are your customers—the most important people in your business. They are not dependent on you, but your income depends on them. Your relations with them will determine your success in the property management business.

You should keep a rental schedule for each month on each of your buildings. This will be sort of a price list for your property. On this schedule, list the names of the tenants that live in each unit, and do your best to keep the list current. As you review the rent schedule and take receipt of rent, make a mental note of the tenants' names. This way when you see them on the property, you can address them properly. This makes tenants feel noticed, and it is great for tenant relations. Encourage your employees, like the general manager and resident manager, to do the same. Always remember that happy residents make money for you. Try to stay on cordial terms with everyone in your building. Everybody likes positive attention, especially from his or her landlord. Be friendly and don't be afraid to strike up small conversations. Small talk has big advantages. Show friendliness and say thanks often.

Whenever you get a complaint, say "I'll check on it right away"—and then follow through. Write the complaint down if it will help you remember and then complete any necessary repairs immediately. If there will be a delay, keep the tenant informed. By attending to each and every complaint, no matter how minor, you will put yourself way ahead of other owners— who are your competition. Far too many tenants have had miserable experiences with their landlords. Do not let yourself fall into this category.

Do You Need a Resident Manager?

Many cities and municipalities require a resident manager only in buildings with sixteen units or more. These rules and regulations differ in various communities, cities, and even states, and it is important to be aware of them. Sometimes, regardless of rules and regulations, it can be handy to have a resident manager who can show vacancies when needed, put out the garbage, and keep up with the yard work, even though you plan to closely oversee the property yourself. Of course, if you live next door or nearby, this might not be necessary. It depends on how convenient the location is for you to get to and how much time you plan to devote to management.

Hire a General Manager

After you have acquired approximately forty units, you can probably afford to put a full-time employee on your payroll. This would take the place of hiring contractors, handymen, and spot labor. Your local bank could even handle payroll, paying necessary taxes, providing W-2s and other statements, and handling additional business-related activities so you can concentrate on operating your properties.

The person you hire should have good handyman skills and a general interest in rehabilitating your apartments. You will also need someone who has both good social skills and street smarts. He or she can act as your general manager and perform duties like the following:

- Selecting tenants for your vacancies
- Collecting rents for your properties
- Performing tenant maintenance requests
- Modernizing, remodeling and otherwise preparing your vacancies for the next tenants (as suggested in chapter 5)

It pays to hire someone who can perform these duties in your place or in place of hiring expensive independent contractors. You can then spend your time overseeing your holdings and searching for good acquisitions. You can look at it this way: Labor that is hired is tax deductible. Your personal labor is not. Many investors fail to make progress because they need to change their ways of operating as they increase their holdings. You can get a good start by doing the work yourself when you begin. But as you grow, you need to delegate as much as possible in order to assure your expansion.

Renting Your Units

If you have just taken over a property and you get notice that someone is going to move, don't panic. Vacancies are a good thing. As highlighted in chapters 5 and 6, vacancies allow you to upgrade units, which in turn allows you to upgrade rents. When you first take over a property, you should almost hope for vacancies because you can fill those units with tenants that you have picked. In all likelihood, you will be getting buildings that already have vacancies.

If an existing tenant intends to leave, be sure to put the "good" in good-bye. Tenants are supposed to give thirty to sixty days' notice to vacate. But many people do not plan far enough ahead to do this. Or it may not be possible to give notice, if, for instance, the person must move for a job or because of other extenuating circumstances. When the tenant does not give notice, you cannot very well force them to stay for the full month. Normally, you would have to work out a proration of the rent amount due.

You should formally check out the old resident, including performing a detailed inspection of the apartment. Most tenants pay a security deposit upon move-in. This is supposed to cover the cost of putting the apartment into rentable condition *after* the tenant moves. If the apartment is vacated in the same condition in which it was rented (less normal usage), you have an obligation to return the deposit. Any portion of the deposit, however, can be used to cover the costs of repairs, replacement, or damage to the apartment. By inspecting units before tenants move out, you can tell them what needs to be done to get their full deposits refunded. Your tenants will appreciate knowing how to get that money back, and taking this step could save you time and money on preparing the unit for the next tenant.

Some owners take advantage of tenants by keeping the full deposit regardless of the condition of the unit; this is unethical and shortsighted. Sooner or later a resident who did not get his deposit back will learn that other people have been getting their deposits from other owners. He will realize that he was shortchanged, and he will talk about it. Word will get around to the detriment of the apartment owner. This type of thing is particularly damaging in a multiple-unit property where tenants have the opportunity to bad-mouth you to each other. So return the deposit. I make it a practice to give the benefit of the doubt to the tenant. He may sincerely believe he left the unit clean. You may disagree with the tenant's assessment, but give the deposit back anyway.

Preparations for the next tenant should start as soon as the previous one disappears down the street. This should take one of two forms. If the unit has not been renovated per chapter 5 on improvements, you will need to gut the entire apartment. If a total remodel has been done within the past few years, you may only need to touch up paint, recarpet, and thoroughly clean the apartment.

Your next task is to get every inch of the apartment sparkling clean. Many managers neglect this, and some will show apartments with dirty carpets, unwashed windows, marks on walls, and grease on kitchen ceilings. There may be dirt on the floor and under the major appliances. Sometimes there are dead insects in the light globes, or the bathroom sink has not been cleaned. Maybe the medicine cabinet shelves are old, rusty, and chipped. Many managers show apartments when bulbs are missing from light fixtures or when the power is off, so the manager has to show the apartment by flashlight. Vacant apartments shown by your competitors are likely to have some of these faults. And their managers tend to say, "We'll fix it before you move in."

What type of tenant do you think is going to move into an apartment with these egregious incompletions? Probably one that can't get accepted anywhere else. More than likely, this is not going to be the most desirable person to have as a tenant.

Owners that show and rent units in this fashion have nothing but problems. It is difficult to collect rents on units in this condition, and your local municipal inspectors may send you a letter citing code violations. You will have nothing but headaches.

Most people try to find a better apartment when they are moving. If a rundown apartment means moving up, just how bad was their last place? You do not want such people in your building.

In prepping your vacancy, make sure everything is working properly and ensure there are no leaky faucets or toilets. Cleaning the apartment in a way that will entice a potential tenant is an art. You can hire a professional cleaning service, have your manager do the cleaning, or perform this task as part of your managerial duties.

In cleaning the unit, you'll want to pay special attention to certain key tasks.

- Clean and wipe out all cupboards and cabinets. Make sure the latches work and the drawers pull out easily.

- Wash the windows inside and out using glass cleaner.
- Wash the windowsills, blinds, and screens. Clean the light switches or simply put on new ones. Take the light fixtures apart and clean them. Check for burned-out bulbs.
- Use TSP (trisodium phosphate, a degreaser) to clean the kitchen and bathroom ceiling and walls.
- In the bathroom, wash the tiles, shower door, tub, soap dish, and plumbing fixtures with hot water and steel wool soap pads. Check if the tub needs caulking. If it does, first clean it, let it dry for 24 hours, and then apply the new caulking compound.
- Replace the toilet seat if it has worn spots. Clean the toilet and water tank. Ensure that the medicine cabinet and mirror are in immaculate condition. Clean and buff the bathroom tile or linoleum using steel wool soap pads.
- Clean the stove and refrigerator or, if necessary, replace them with new or reconditioned appliances. Scrub the floors with steel wool soap pads. Clean the sink and countertop. Check for leaks under the sink. Clean the area under the sink cabinet. Vacuum the drawers and cabinets. Polish the kitchen faucet. Clean the hood over the stove, and replace the hood screen with a new one.
- After you have done all of the above, remove all of your cleaning supplies except your vacuum cleaner, which you will use for a final cleaning of the carpet.

Now that you have thoroughly cleaned the unit, keep a key, and inspect it daily until it is rented. Make sure your resident manager and general manager have a key also. Label the key so there is no delay in showing it to a potential tenant, who can appear at any time. Inspecting the apartment daily will protect you against unpleasant surprises like bugs and leaks.

Advertising Vacancies

If you know the unit is in tip-top shape, you will have the confidence to ask for top rent from new tenants. You will attract quality tenants and be ahead of your competition. The key now is to let people know that you have vacancies. If your building is located on a busy street, the "for rent" sign that you have posted on the front of your building can be very effective in getting the attention of potential tenants. Do not hang a sign that embarrasses you or your building. Have it professionally made with eye-catching colors. Make sure your sign is always clean and properly lit. It should be visible to people approaching the property—that is, at right angles to traffic, not parallel. Also, if you have off-street parking, mention it on the sign since many tenants care more about their cars than anything else.

While we are on the topic of signs, I'll say a few words about the types of signs that should not be on your buildings. Many property owners and managers like to post signs that say, "KEEP OFF THE GRASS" or "QUIET AFTER 10 PM." This is not the type of atmosphere you want to maintain. If you have a specific problem with residents doing something undesirable, the best way to handle it is to distribute typed memos to *ALL* tenants explaining the situation and asking for compliance with the rules. This keeps the issue out of the public perception and also avoids singling out any one tenant specifically.

Maintaining the landscaping of your building in a neat, attractive fashion is also important. The lawn should be green (if possible) and well kept. If your manager cannot keep it up because of lack of time or interest, then hire a gardener. Make sure that the main features of your yard are not crabgrass, dandelions, cigarette butts, and gum wrappers. In my experience, well-maintained landscaping can increase occupancy by about 5 percent on average. A nurseryman or landscape gardener will probably be glad to tell you what will grow attractively on the property.

Prospects who walk in off the street just because they have seen your sign and liked the looks of your place may be enough to keep your building fully rented. Still, you will find yourself wasting a lot of time on unqualified candidates who do not want what you have or who are undesirable. You need to be extremely careful in sizing up these strangers and checking their references to make sure you don't get stuck with oddballs, misfits, or other problem people. This includes people who habitually break leases, move every few months, or are constantly late with their rent payments. All of this can be verified by checking references. Just one bad guess in renting can be costly.

Often, talking with prospects referred by someone you know is much easier. Through a mutual acquaintance, you already have a rough idea of what the person is like. These candidates also probably know that your apartments are what they want. These kinds of referrals can be facilitated through flyer distribution (as discussed in chapter 5) to advertise your vacancies. If you place flyers at businesses in which you know the owner, you will have a built-in recommendation source.

Free advertising may be the best. Everyone living in your building is a potential source of advertisement. They know your building, currently live in the apartments, and presumably like them. Your best prospects are those who get interested because of recommendations from people who already live there. Setting up referral bonuses for current tenants can help immeasurably with this.

Other areas for free referral sources besides your own building include nearby markets, pharmacies, Laundromats, and other community gathering places that have public bulletin boards where you can place your flyers to advertise your vacancies.

There really is no set rule of thumb that will tell you how long it will take to fill your vacancies. There are too many factors to consider. Some areas get overbuilt, while other areas get hit by business reversals, such as the closing of a major employer, which instigates massive layoffs in the area.

If word of mouth, your vacancy sign, flyers posted in your neighborhood, and web postings on websites such as Craigslist.com are not attracting qualified tenants, you may need to run a classified ad in your local paper. In many metropolitan areas, this ad will be placed on the paper's website as well. Many people say classified ads are old-fashioned, but they are still effective in attracting qualified applicants to your vacant apartments.

When listing your amenities, try to use words that are powerfully descriptive, such as *spacious, attractive, plush, luxurious, modern, comfortable, convenient, beautiful, sparkling* or *secluded*. These adjectives will get prospects' attention. Basically, your ad should encourage the prospective tenant to call the number listed. These key words, the price of the apartment, and the number of bedrooms should all help to facilitate this goal.

Most metropolitan areas have one daily newspaper that is the obvious leader in apartment ads. They may even have a special weekly section devoted to apartment listings. That is the newspaper you want to be in. If you are in a suburban area, however, you may need to test several local papers. Be sure to try the weekly community papers and shopping guides. Sometimes they pull better prospects than the big dailies. As with anything, trial and error will uncover what best works for you.

Sunday advertising is still very important. The Sunday paper is normally the biggest edition of the week and the one most newspaper readers try to read. Because of this, it is also the day most prospects are looking. But you should also run one or two weekday ads to maximize your coverage. Your weekday ads can be shorter than your Sunday ad because there will be fewer ads competing against you. Also, I have found that someone who looks for apartments during the week is a more serious shopper than a Sunday prospect.

When your potential tenants call, you must make a good impression via the telephone. The telephone may be more important than anything else in your business. People judge by first impressions, and those who call get their first impressions of you through that initial phone contact. Many may never come to see the apartment if they don't like what they hear in that first phone conversation.

You or your manager needs to sell your vacancy to anyone who calls because of your sign, ads, or flyers. Be sure to recite the amenities of your apartment and building, and do so before waiting for the prospect to ask. Also make sure that you tell them when you are available to show it, rather than simply waiting for them to ask to see it. You want to do everything possible to encourage your prospects to feel at ease. Your goal is to invite them out to meet you and see what you are offering, so as you can tell, it is crucial for you to make a good impression via the telephone. If you fail, your previous efforts to market your vacancy lose their full effectiveness.

Once your prospect has committed to an appointment to see your vacancy, you can start to feel as though you have accomplished your goal.

This signals to you that it is time to end the conversation, so invite them to continue it in person. That tells prospective tenants that you want to talk to them more, which is inviting.

Choosing a Tenant

Some owners and managers think that the rent-paying ability of the resident is the sole standard they should consider in choosing a new tenant. You will do much better by renting to residents who are desirable by other standards as well. You want to be sure that a given prospect will fit in with the other residents in your building. For example, you may not want to rent to a young, twentysomething "kid" who is moving out of his parents house for the first time when the rest of your tenants are near retirement age. This invites a social and cultural clash and can cause major headaches down the line. Find a tenant that fits, and everyone will be more compatible and stay longer. The residents you select will—more than anything else—determine the success or failure of your investment. Always remember that.

Once potential tenants show up to see your vacancies, you should probe to see how long they have had their current apartments. At least two years in the same place would be desirable. This goes for employment as well. The longer the better, but at least two years is acceptable. You should always wait for a prospect to fill out a rental application and check out his references before jumping to most conclusions, but your first casual questions can sometimes uncover warning signals. Someone on a payroll is usually a safer candidate than someone whose income is irregular. Wages can be garnished, if need be, to collect rent. This is not to say that many people fail to pay their rent; but it is just one of the possibilities you should think about in choosing the best available applicant for your apartments. If the prospect is self-employed, do not be afraid to ask for more seasoning in their income (more than two years). Again, a tenant who is unable to pay the rent is not the tenant that you want for your investment.

As a general rule of thumb, you should select applicants who earn at least three times the rent. Some applicants may want to give you their rent and deposit on the spot. As tempting as this might be, you must tell them you need a few days to review their application. You need to be cautious in these situations as your new would-be occupant might be getting evicted from his current apartment. If that were the case, you would certainly want to know why. In any event, should you rent to someone with an eviction on his or her record? I would advise you to look at it in a situational fashion. If it was because of job loss and they have now recovered, you may want to rent to them. Keep in mind that a tenant who is bad for one owner might turn out to be fine for another under firmer collection and operating policies. An eviction may have the effect of making a tenant more responsible thereafter.

Should you run credit checks on prospective candidates? Many owners prefer to use their own judgment to size up prospects. Operate according to your own preference on this, but certainly you should check court records for prior evictions. Personally, I have found that most potential occupants have either no recorded credit or poor credit. With Section 8 applicants, you would not need a credit report because the housing authority pays their rent. If the applicant is employed and on Section 8, and subsequently loses his or her job, the housing authority normally steps in to make up for the loss of their rental portion.

When you have found a candidate who is interested in your vacancy, give the person an application to complete. You can obtain typical apartment house rental applications from your local apartment owners association.

Some applicants will want to take the application home; others will fill it out on the spot. Either way is acceptable. If they have suitable employment income, and you are comfortable with them, then they are probably worthwhile to rent to.

If you wait for the perfect tenant to show up, you will more than likely have lots of empty apartments to show. In my personal estimation, 98 percent of the applicants you choose will be good tenants. You certainly will not be right all of the time. But if your buildings are maintained and in excellent condition, you will attract the type of people you want to rent to in the first place, and your selection process will begin at a higher level.

You should not accept anyone as your tenant who has not completely filled out the application. The potential tenant's business address and occupation, along with other basic information, should prove helpful in screening any doubts you may have about the candidate. These details will also prove invaluable if you have to take action later to collect delinquent rent or other damages. You should also have this information in order to know whom to notify in case of a tenant's death or serious illness.

Once you have decided to rent to a prospect, you should check out the application in a timely fashion. This process should not take more than two days; otherwise you may lose your potential tenant. Once the applicant has been approved, call the would-be tenant to inform him or her that the rental application has been approved. You will then need to explain that the entire first month's rent and full deposit are due before the keys will be handed over. Also, it is far better to prorate the second month of tenancy than the first.

In the event the prospect would like for you to hold the apartment for them until the first of the following month, then ask for a deposit to do so. Most of the time, when this comes up, it is because the prospective tenant needs to give his current landlord reasonable notice that he is moving. If the prospect gives you a holding deposit, it is likely that he will return to pay the balance of the deposit and first month's rent in order to obtain the keys and move in.

It is always good to ask for one full month of rent and a deposit before the tenant moves in. For example, if the monthly rent is $850 and the deposit is $850, the total move-in amount due would be $1,700. If the tenant wants to move in on the fifteenth of the month and he pays $1,700 to move in, the rent due on the following first of the month would be 50 percent of the rent (i.e., $425). By paying the full rent and deposit, tenants demonstrate to you their commitment to becoming your occupants.

Many potential tenants will ask if they can split up payment of the security deposit; in other words, they may want to pay half of the security deposit at move-in and the other half in thirty days. Usually this does not work, as the tenant really has no incentive to pay the balance after moving in. Always collect the security deposit and the first month's rent *before* giving the keys to your prospect. Prospects routinely ask me to split the deposit, so I assume there are many managers who allow this method of payment. I try to avoid it, as I am concerned that it may set a bad precedent for the future behavior of the new tenant. However, if you operate in an area where the rental market is soft, you may need to arrange for such payments in order to maintain reasonable occupancy in your building.

When your new tenant pays the stipulated move-in amounts, you should take the opportunity to review and sign your written lease or rental agreement. Oral terms concerning the rental of property are generally legal when handled on a month-to-month basis. Leasing for more than a year, as with the sale of real estate, must be in writing to be binding.

Many property owners handle all rentals on an oral basis, which means that their only protection against undesirable tenants is applicable state or municipal laws.

The more successful operator requires a written contract on each rental unit. Besides providing a safeguard against undesirables, this ensures that each tenant understands the terms of the agreement for the general benefit of all the tenants in the building.

Some owners disapprove of written agreements because they fear that they grant additional rights to tenants, but it's important to understand that the written lease is intended to clarify the terms between owner and tenant. For the tenant it confirms, for the most part, the protection already provided by the law. For the owner, the lease includes safeguards over and above those granted by law.

Important paragraphs of a typical lease include the following.

- Lessor/Lessee names
- Whether it is a term lease or a month-to-month lease
- Amount of monthly rent
- Amount of deposit paid
- Due date of rent and corresponding late charges
- Purpose and use of the refundable security deposit.
- Outline of house rules

- Who is permitted to occupy the apartment
- Explanation of the owner's "right of entry and inspection"

Be sure to review the lease with your tenant thoroughly and have him sign it. I have found that most tenants do not read rental agreements, so you need to go over the highlights.

If you have more than one property, the leases should be filed by separate properties and by rental units at each property. It is advisable to retain these rental agreements for at least two years after a tenant vacates in case questions arise later or you need to provide a listing of rental income for refinancing purposes. In addition, keeping rental agreements can serve as a check on turnover in each unit; excessive turnover would indicate a need for improvements.

How to Collect Rents When Due

Income rental operations demand full rent collections when due. It is better to have a vacant apartment unit with no tenant, eliminating the costs of wear and tear, than to have a tenant who does not pay. Operating apartments must be viewed as a moneymaking investment and not charity. Once you blur that line, you may never clarify it again.

Rent collection will be more efficient if consistent collection steps and proper notices and forms are utilized. Always give each tenant a receipt for rent paid. Use a rent receipt book that makes duplicate copies (available from any office supply store). By making a duplicate of each receipt, you keep a copy of every receipt that you give your tenants. This will help to alleviate future arguments that may arise about whether or not rent was paid and what time period the payment covered. When owners fail to give receipts, tenants can claim they are paid up or that they have paid a month ahead. Try to have your manager make out the receipts in advance, as things around the building can become busy during the first five days of each month. Your manager could be busy filling vacancies and collecting rent; thus, if the receipts are prepared in advance, the risk of making a mistake can be substantially reduced.

Most tenants expect to pay their rent faithfully on the due date as a primary obligation. For those with slow payment habits and particularly for new tenants, certain educational steps can be very effective. If rent is not paid when it is due, no action should be taken until the following day. On the evening of the second day, the manager should contact the tenant and ask if he is ready to pay the rent. The manager must get all rents promptly collected and turned over to the owner. If the tenant is not home, the manager should leave a note under the tenant's door requesting that the tenant call the manager.

Some—especially those who pay the rent—may question such prompt reminder action. You should simply explain that the rents are due on or about the first of every month. If that is an inconvenience for the tenant, explain that you would be glad to change the date and prorate the rent to adjust for the change. You can be flexible and firm at the same time. Remember that.

How to Handle Bad Tenants

Most of the tenants you choose to rent to will be honest, respectable people who pay their rent on time and mind their own business. But even if you adhere to the careful screening steps described earlier in this chapter, you may not be able to prevent the occasional deadbeat or troublemaker from getting into your building.

Just one malicious tenant in your apartment house can keep the entire building in turmoil. An undesirable tenant can turn happy tenants into dissatisfied ones. Contented tenants will eventually turn sour and vacate unless you throw out the troublemaker. In order to keep your building full and running smoothly, you need to operate with specific policies and house rules.

Good service and value for your tenants is not always enough to keep things smooth between you and them. As a manager, you will meet some characters that you would not ordinarily come into contact with. They will test you to see whether or not they can handle you. As you develop a reputation for being able to handle them, you will be tested less. The better you handle people, the more you will prosper. For me, the situation in which I have historically encountered bad tenants is with new acquisitions. As described in chapter 6, most of the properties I purchase are in dire need of attention, with respect to both repairs and management. If you are buying property in need of improvement, you are probably going to inherit the sloppy operating practices of the former owner—and that may include some shady tenants. You will need to know how best to remove continuously difficult people who wreck your plans. To review, your screening procedures for your vacancies should include the following steps:

- Ensure that apartments for rent are clean, modernized, and in tip-top shape.
- Obtain a fully completed rental application.
- Check for any past evictions.
- Verify current employment.
- Check past landlord history.
- Confirm exactly who will be renting the unit. (How many will be living in the apartment?)
- Obtain the full deposit and first month's rent before handing over the keys.
- Have your next occupant sign your rental agreement and house rules.

Other than judiciously applying the above procedures, there is not much more that an owner can do to screen applicants. More than likely, you will have very few problems. However, when you do encounter a deadbeat or troublemaker, you need to take action immediately. You also need to be particularly vigilant in dealing with any drug activity in or around your buildings.

So How Do You Get Them Out?

I have described steps you can take to extract rent from slow-paying tenants simply by being vigilant in enforcing your operating procedures. But none of those steps work when confronting a deadbeat—someone who won't or can't pay you. Your only recourse is to evict those tenants, just as this is your only recourse with people who pay their rent but are troublemakers in other ways.

Some owners hesitate to start evicting tenants because the process is costly and troublesome when done the legal way. Sometimes they postpone action when a nonpaying resident says something like, "I'll pay you when my check comes in next Friday." If these are new occupants, or if you have had previous difficulties in collection from them, you had better stand firm and evict.

A manager who enables his or her residents to fall behind in rent will soon find them even further behind. The tenant may realize it is easier to skip paying back rent altogether, rather than pay a combined amount that seems astronomical. If the tenant can't pay one month, how can he pay two? It is not fair to your other tenants when they work hard to pay you and you let someone slide in their responsibilities to you.

You can allow a little leeway if the tenant has a past record of reliability; but even then, do not accept a vague assurance like, "I'll take care of it as soon as I can." Establish firm pay dates and amounts. Dates and dollars are what you are interested in, and the agreed-upon date should be no more than five days in the future. You can say, "I'll hold off on legal action on the understanding that you will make full payment by Friday." But don't delay if they fail to make the payment by the promised date. Take action to get them out.

Evicting a tenant the right way takes four to eight weeks. If your tenant is sophisticated in delaying an eviction, the process can take up to four months or longer; this is why owners charge such lofty deposits.

Never try to evict outside the legal process. You will be sued if you enter the tenant's premises without permission, change his locks, or remove a door. And don't think you'll be protected by a rental agreement that says those tactics are allowed. Such agreements are void in most states.

Before starting a legal eviction, you might be able to talk the tenant out the door. You would be surprised how many people will take the money and go if you offer to return their deposit in full in exchange for them handing over the keys. Buying out an undesirable tenant is often the simplest and cheapest solution to the problem. This is true even though you may hate the idea of throwing good money after bad. The alternative can be much more expensive, in terms of both dollars and time.

When you have rented to an undesirable and you cannot buy him out, the first step to evicting the tenant is serving a written three-day notice. This is used when someone is in arrears in rent, although it can be amended to work in other situations in which eviction may be necessary. The notice can be something as simple as a note that reads, "Three-day notice to shut off loud noise after 10:00 PM or leave."

The usual cases for eviction are actual violations of the rental agreement, such as nonpayment of rent, creating a nuisance, or violating other house rules, which a resident signed a promise to obey.

The three-day notice always gives the occupant an alternative to moving. It implies that, if he meets your demand, he is entitled to stay. This is almost the only kind of notice that you can personally hand to the resident, fasten to his door, or mail to him as a last resort. Other legal papers must be served by a third party, such as a sheriff, court-appointed officer, or process server.

The object of the notice is to force the tenant to move, make good on a provision of the rental agreement, or pay rent owed. It warns the tenant and gives him a chance to make good. The notice should include these details:

- Tenant's name
- Address of rental unit
- Amount of delinquent rent or specific violation of rental agreement provision
- Date of serving notice
- Name of individual on whom notice is served

These forms can be obtained from your local or state apartment house association. In all cases you will need to retain the original copy of the notice in the event that court action is required.

Serving one of these notices must precede any court action that you will need to complete. The court action is called unlawful detainer; it is the legal method used to remove tenants from your property. It pays to pursue any legitimate course of action that gets the tenant out of your building before engaging in legal action. When and if you get to this point, you will have to consult an attorney.

On nonpayment of rent, if you accept any portion of the delinquent rent stated in your three-day notice, you will need to rewrite the notice and serve an updated notice on your tenant. Also if your tenant offers you the amount stated in the notice within the three days, you are obligated by law to accept it. If your tenant offers the amount to you after the expiration of the three-day notice, you are not obligated to accept it. If your attorney starts an unlawful detainer (an eviction) and your tenant offers any portion of the delinquent rent—and you accept it—your attorney is obligated to dismiss the court action. But keep in mind that, once the unlawful detainer is commenced, you are not obligated to accept any rent, just as you are not obligated to accept any rent after expiration of the three-day notice. This is something to keep in mind.

Sometimes you can talk people out the door with a thirty-day notice of termination. First prepare a thirty-day notice form. Present this to your tenant and be prepared for a variety of reactions, including tears or maybe even the threat of violence. Avoid all friction if you can. Keep chatting to a minimum during the interaction. Be polite but definite, and get to the point quickly. Tell the tenant that he won't want an eviction on his record and therefore should cooperate with you.

When seeking to pressure a troublemaker (but not a deadbeat) to leave, a tactic that you can try is raising the undesirable's rent. This avoids the unpleasant interview and the "get out" notice described above. In addition, the tenant can save face, telling everyone that he would rather move than pay the higher rent.

But if he does not pay, he may be able to stall you for another few months before being evicted. He may even pay the raised rent for a while, continuing to cause trouble until he finds another apartment.

If your community has rent control, you will need to be certain you are operating within the rent control law when serving a thirty-day notice to terminate tenancy or when raising an undesirable's rent. Many rent controls reduce the justifications for forcing someone to move and limit your rent increases. You should get a copy of the law and see how it applies to your case.

You will need to get court help if an occupant still refuses to vacate after receiving your notice to do so. As previously stated, unlawful detainer cases are usually handled by local attorneys. Your attorney will need the original copy of your notice—with proof of service—and an original copy of the rental agreement. Expect the process to take four to eight weeks.

Of course, all of this is a worst-case scenario. If you are careful in the selection of your tenants in the beginning and if you only rent sparkling-clean, up-to-date apartments, you will seldom need to go through an eviction.

One final point: often the fastest and easiest method of getting an undesirable tenant out is to offer the person a cash incentive to move.

Chapter Recap

Property management is people management.

- Keep your tenants happy and treat them well in an effort to keep turnover low. When you see them, refer to them by name.
- Consider paying a responsible tenant in the property to show vacancies and keep the property clean.
- When your operations expand, consider hiring a general manager.
- When you have a vacancy, assess whether or not it should be remodeled (as per chapter 5) or simply cleaned thoroughly.
- Heavily advertise your vacancies with signs, flyers, print advertising, and the Internet.
- In choosing a tenant, your personal judgment counts heavily.
- When you have a problem with a tenant, consider offering cash to encourage the person to move.

-8-

How to Buy a Single-Family Home

In the game of life it's a good idea to have a few early losses, which relieves you of the pressure of trying to maintain an undefeated season.

—Bill Vaughan, columnist

A single-family house is usually the first property type most realty investors buy. Of all real estate investments, rented houses are probably the easiest to buy and sell. With just a small cash investment, you can easily acquire a property and start your career as a real estate tycoon.

If you choose to rent your house, rather than live in it, you can personally handle whatever problems arise with your tenant. You can keep the books, write checks for repairs and maintenance, and do certain chores yourself. All of this will give you part-time experience in property management, which is good background for more ambitious realty investments.

Depending on your level of talent and spare time, you may or may not evaluate a house in terms of what you can do to fix it up. There are plenty of possibilities to rehabilitate houses and resell at good profits for amateurs with building or interior design skills. The key to this is choosing decent neighborhoods.

Stories abound about how people bought dilapidated houses, spent their spare time renovating them inside and out, sold them for profits of 50 percent or more, and found that they enjoyed the projects so much that

155

they retired from their day jobs and made full-time businesses of buying and refurbishing houses for resale. This works very well in an expanding economy. But when a housing recession hits, as it does about every ten years or so, houses stop selling, and historically, mortgage money tends to dry up. This was certainly the case during the 1980–82 recession, in which interest rates rose as high as 20 percent. It was difficult to sell a property for cash. The 1990–91 recession witnessed the demise of many of the country's savings and loan institutions. The Resolution Trust Corporation was created by Congress to sell REOs (real estate owned, or foreclosed property owned by banks), which depressed property values everywhere. The relatively mild recession of 2000–01 had little effect on the housing industry, but the financial crisis of 2008, of course, was devastating to many people. You need to be aware of what you are getting into. This is simply another reason that income properties can be so valuable. The monthly income of these investments continues, despite bumps in the economy.

In addition to the tax shelter—which is proportionately the same as for an apartment house—the average investor buys a single-family house mainly for the appreciation, not the monthly income.

When you buy a single-family house, you are primarily buying the resale value. Whoever you resell it to will probably live in it. They will be much more concerned about the location than a renter would be. For these reasons, you want to buy in a neighborhood that is up and coming. Ask local shopkeepers whether there are rumors of any large developments in the pipeline. Also, have conversations with the local municipal clerks. Local city employees can tell you how strictly they enforce their zoning codes. You certainly wouldn't want to buy into a neighborhood where homes are in danger of turning into seedy rooming houses or nursing homes. You want a location that will keep its character. Strict zoning ordinances and building codes ensure that your desired location will keep its stability.

Be sure to ask about taxes when you talk to municipal employees. Don't just rely on general tax rates published by the city or state. Real estate taxes often vary widely from one locality to the next. You need to find out about all local taxes and assessments, not just real estate taxes. This can be important in an outlying area where you could find yourself assessed extra fees to pay for new streets, curbs, sidewalks, or sewers.

How to Find a Single-Family Bargain

When looking for single-family homes to purchase for investment purposes, your objective should be to find properties that you can buy for about 20 percent less than market value, much like in the search for apartment buildings. This gives you a margin of safety to work within. It takes lots of work and imagination, and you must realize that only about 2 percent of the properties on the market at any given time will meet your criteria.

We frequently see everyday people in the news who have been hit by hard times. People lose their jobs, or payments on their adjustable mortgage loans rise too high for them to afford. The homes that people in these difficult circumstances are selling may be in need of repairs that they cannot afford to make. I have known owners of single-family homes whose properties were so old and outdated that they could not find decent renters for them. Or if these owners did find renters for their houses, the tenants did not stay long. Such turnover can wear out an owner, especially if it has been occurring for many years.

Some sellers underprice their properties because they do not know how much similar properties have been selling for recently. Or they may not be aware of unique advantages that favorably separate their properties from others.

Another source of potential good buys is property listings that have been on the market for a while, say, at least three or four months. By this time, the seller's agent has probably reduced the price a couple of times, and the owner may be ready to accept a below-market offer.

Older owners who have lived in their houses for several decades may be willing to entertain your offer. In some cases it will have been many years since they made improvements to the property. The property could be in such poor condition that no one is interested in buying.

Newspapers, Internet listings, and other publications can help you find bargain properties. Call realtors to obtain information, and when a property sounds promising, set up a meeting with the broker to view it. Be sure to thoroughly read the ads for houses for rent. This will help you to determine rent levels in various locations and neighborhoods. Then zero in on ads that refer to a "lease-option" or that indicate the houses are "for rent or sale." These kinds of ads generally indicate a flexible and motivated seller.

It is also important to look beyond real estate ads in your search for bargains. You can identify potential sellers from public notices; divorces, retirements, deaths, bankruptcy, and foreclosures all may cause people to seek to sell homes. Each of these events can force the need to sell real estate. If you contact these potential sellers before they list with a broker, you stand a good chance of buying at a good price.

What about Foreclosures?

In recent years, the news media has given the topic of home foreclosures plenty of coverage. In order to take advantage of the profit opportunities that can be gained from foreclosures, you need to know how the foreclosure process works.

Simply put, in most cases, borrowers default because they fail to make their mortgage payments. But defaults can also occur when owners fail to pay their property taxes, homeowners association fees, or special assessments; transfer mortgaged properties without lender approval; or begin renovations, remodeling, or demolition that diminishes the value of the property.

Most lenders today give delinquent borrowers generous opportunities to restructure or refinance their mortgages. The delinquency problem can be a huge burden for banks.

In order to mitigate (somewhat) massive dumping of homes on the housing market, banks have stepped up their efforts to encourage short sales. A short sale is when a buyer offers less for a home than the outstanding principal balance on the existing mortgage secured by the property. In some markets, short sales represent 20 percent or more of current sales. This is up from about 10 percent four years ago. Some banks are now even offering their borrowers cash incentives to encourage a short sale. These cash incentives are paid after close of escrow and can be used for relocation expenses or other purposes.

When a lender finally gives up on a pre-foreclosure workout, it files either a legal notice of default or a lawsuit to foreclose, depending on the state. This legal filing at the county recorder's office and the subsequent posting of notices on the Internet or in newspapers formally announces to the property owners, any other parties who may have claims against the owners or their property, and the general public that action is moving forward to force a "courthouse" sale of the property.

During the waiting period (normally sixty to 120 days), the lender hopes that someone will step forward and either buy the property or reinstate the loan. Often a short sale can be arranged during this period, whereby the lender agrees to take less than the principal balance owing on the loan.

Eventually, when the defaulting owners run out of delaying tactics, the foreclosure date arrives. The property is auctioned to the highest cash bidder. Sometimes a real estate investor, speculator, or even a homebuyer may submit the winning bid, but more commonly, the lender who has forced the foreclosure sale bids, say, one dollar more than the unpaid claims (mortgage balance, late fees, interest, and costs of foreclosure) and walks away with a trustee's deed to the property, thereby becoming the new owner and making the property an REO property.

There are three methods by which you can obtain a below-market deal with foreclosures:

- Negotiating with the defaulting owners and, if necessary, the foreclosing lenders (You might obtain a short sale and/or refinance this way.)
- Bidding at the foreclosure auction
- Buying an REO (real estate owned) from the lender or the insuring agency (The owner of the property would be FHA, VA, or Fannie Mae and Freddie Mac.)

Buying from a Defaulting Homeowner

When the housing market is down, buying foreclosed homes is always an option. You can sometimes get a home in a short sale or for much less than the market value. Many investors build their businesses by buying foreclosed property. Another upside to buying a preforeclosure from a distressed owner is that you can sometimes salvage the owner's credit record (and part of his home equity), and at the same time secure a bargain for yourself. Distressed property owners sometimes accept an offer for a quick close of escrow at a price that is less than market value.

While this seems like an ideal situation for an investor to take advantage of, it can sometimes backfire. The reality is that, in dealing with owners in foreclosure, you are likely to run across a multitude of problems. One problem is the fact that few mortgages today permit assumptions. To put it bluntly, if your credit or income is less than stellar, or if you plan to flip the property without taking occupancy or to hold the property as a rental, many mortgage holders will not let you assume an existing mortgage. This means that you will have to secure new financing in your name or in the name of your entity, which can lead to fees, credit checks, and long closing times.

Property owners who suffer foreclosures often get hit by additional claims from other creditors; these could include tax liens or secured judgments against the homeowners. In order to clear the title, you would need to clean up and settle with several creditors—not just the one mortgage lender.

You will probably find that most homeowners who contend with foreclosure owe more than their properties are worth, so to make a deal work, you must talk the lender into a short sale. In a short sale, the lender voluntarily reduces the balance due on the loan so that you have some incentive for agreeing to make up past-due payments and take over the loan. Today more and more lenders are using this method to help alleviate the foreclosure crisis, as they are starting to realize that this avenue will cost them less in the long run. You must realize, however, that almost all bankers hate to reduce or waive any principal loan amounts. As a result, you may get the runaround, wait a long time to get a decision, and then sometimes lose the entire deal to a higher bidder. Another issue you need to concern yourself with is whether the homeowner can convey marketable title, that is, a title free of other liens on the property. Do not forget to factor in any outstanding property taxes that are owed.

You should also establish how much you must spend to repair and renovate the property.

Bid at a Foreclosure Auction

Almost all foreclosure sales lose money for lenders, lien holders, and property owners. Foreclosure properties sell at prices much lower than their market values because court auctions do not satisfy the criteria of market-value transactions. The auction sellers provide potential buyers with no information about properties other than their legal descriptions; and there are no title guarantees. The sales require all cash within twenty-four hours; and there are no contracts to allow buyers time to arrange financing. Buyers cannot even guarantee that the property will be vacant.

The risk, expense, and general aggravation of foreclosure sales deter investors and, especially, homeowners from showing up to bid. This is a category best left to professionals who specialize in these auctions.

Even if you put together enough information to manage the risks of buying a foreclosure, you face the problem of coming up with cash for the entire purchase price. After the foreclosure paperwork clears and you get a trustee's deed, you could probably line up a normal mortgage on the property. In the interim though, to buy the property on the steps of the courthouse, you would need to arrange standby credit with your bank, probably a commercial signature loan that you would repay from proceeds of a normal mortgage on the property.

For these and other reasons, very few real estate investors or foreclosure specialists bid on these foreclosure sales. In many cases the properties simply revert back to the foreclosing lenders, and they become the owners.

You should know that foreclosure opportunities expand and diminish as real estate markets weaken or strengthen. In strong markets when the economy is robust, foreclosure bargains become more difficult to locate.

Cyclical downturns, like what we are experiencing as I write this, provide many opportunities for foreclosure buyers.

REOs (Real Estate Owned by Lenders)

Most of today's foreclosures came into the banks' inventories from the subprime loan crisis over the past few years. Sales of these REOs at distressed prices account for much of the general drop in property prices. It has been estimated that at least 30 percent of property transactions in many markets can be attributed to REO and short sales. As REOs pile up, even sellers free of financial distress must cut their prices to compete.

If you are a buyer in this market, the benefit is that you can buy properties today at prices that are 20 to 50 percent off their peak of a few years ago. As the economy begins to right itself over the next few years (and history tells us it will), the high number of REOs that now crowd the market will gradually disappear and fall back to much lower levels. Their depressing effect on market prices will dissipate. We can expect that new housing starts (builds) will remain near historic lows until prices rise substantially above replacement costs. (This prediction is based on historical evidence of the cyclical nature of the real estate market.)

In buying an REO from a bank or private finance company, you do not face the same risks you encounter when buying at a foreclosure auction. In almost all cases, the lenders clean up title problems, pay past-due property taxes, and evict any remaining tenants or occupants. REO lenders may permit you to write contingency offers subject to appraisal, financing, and inspections. REO lenders can serve as sources of built-in financing as well.

Your best bet for finding REOs will probably be to follow up on specific properties after court-ordered foreclosure sales. In other words, in your hunt for properties you may find one that is in foreclosure; simply follow it until the foreclosure is completed. Another potential source could be realtors who specialize in REO listings.

You may also want to inquire at the REO departments of various banks. These days many lenders are overwhelmed with foreclosures, and some do not know what they are doing. With a little persistence, though, you can find a property that will meet your criteria.

If you are not able to buy directly from the lender, the lender may direct you to a realtor who specializes in selling that lender's REOs. You will find, for example, that HUD, the VA, Fannie Mae, and Freddie Mac almost always sell their REOs through brokers. As a rule, banks want to downplay their inventory of REOs so as not to invite unfavorable publicity. They also want to promote good relations with brokers in their communities; ideally, these local realtors will bring them future loan business.

HUD Foreclosures

Each year the FHA (Federal Housing Administration), a division of HUD (the Department of Housing and Urban Development), insures hundreds of thousands of new mortgage loans. If a borrower fails to repay an FHA-insured loan, the owner of the mortgage may force the property into a foreclosure sale. Rather than keep the property in its REO portfolio, the lender turns in a claim to HUD, which then pays the lender the amount due under its mortgage insurance coverage and acquires the foreclosed property. HUD then puts the property—along with all the others it has acquired—up for sale to the general public.

In the context of HUD homes, of which there are many, HUD favors owner-occupants over investors. Owner-occupants get the first right to bid, and HUD offers "low or nothing down" FHA-insured mortgages only to owner-occupants of one- to four-family properties. HUD does not presently finance HUD homes for those who do not intend to live in them. And do not even think about lying to the government and pretending that you plan to live in a home that you are buying purely as an investment property. But if you are looking for a fixer-upper, you can find great HUD buys because first-time homebuyers (HUD's primary market) are reluctant to buy homes that require repairs.

Because it is a government agency, HUD does not make buying simple. Unlike a private purchase in which you write out your offer on any valid contract form, HUD requires a specific contract submission package;

only HUD-approved forms and documentation are allowed. And your contract package must arrive in HUD's regional office according to the department's posted schedule.

Given HUD's well-known inflexibility, it pays to work only with brokers who know the details of HUD's requirements.

Department of Veterans Affairs (VA) Foreclosures

Although the Department of Veteran Affairs (the VA) follows rules similar to HUD, investors gain more from the VA in two ways:

- The VA gives equal status to investors and looks for the highest offer from homeowner to investor.
- Unlike HUD, the VA offers financing to investors. You do not need to be a veteran, and you can get in for a low down payment. The VA typically applies relaxed qualifying credit standards.

Fannie Mae and Freddie Mac REOs

These two agencies are among the largest players in the nation's secondary mortgage market. Fannie Mae and Freddie Mac don't make loans directly to buyers, but they do provide the loan funding for more than 50 percent of the purchases of one- to four-family properties that are financed by other mortgage lenders.

When these loans go bad, Fannie or Freddie may force the lender to buy back its loan, leaving the primary lender with a foreclosed property in its REO portfolio. Usually, though, lenders who faithfully met Fannie or Freddie's underwriting guidelines can require Fannie or Freddie to take ownership of the foreclosed property.

Fannie and Freddie do not use the sealed-bid sales procedures that are common to HUD and the VA. Instead, both companies choose a realty firm and give that firm an exclusive right-to-sell listing. In some circumstances, Fannie and Freddie may spend thousands of dollars to fix up the property upon the recommendation of the realty firm. However, because of the thousands of REOs that the two agencies hold, giving much attention to any individual property is impossible. You will likely find some bargains, and both companies offer favorable financing to credit-qualified investors and homebuyers.

Probate and Estate Sales

Probate and estate sales represent another source of bargain-priced property. When people die, their properties may be sold to satisfy the deceased's mortgage holder and other creditors. Even if there are no pressing creditor concerns, most heirs prefer to sell property rather than keep it. Often times the deceased person has lived in the property for decades; in these cases, the property may be so rundown that it would be impossible to sell at true market value. In many of these situations you can get quite a bargain.

To buy a property through probate you need to submit a bid through the estate's administrator (usually a lawyer) or executor. The probate judge assigned to the case then reviews all bids. Depending on local laws, the judge may then select a bid for approval or reopen the bidding. All of this may depend upon the property's appraisal. Bidding on probate properties can require a lot of fortitude because of the associated delays and legal procedures. Judges act based on the best interests of the estate, and are not driven by market prices or demand. They have wide discretion to accept bids or open up additional rounds of bidding. Your only recourse in these cases is to make your bid and then wait.

Selecting a Single-Family Home

During the boom years of the housing market, speculators made plenty of money by simply buying almost any property, holding it for a predetermined time, and then reselling it for a profit. Those days are long gone.

There are still substantial profits to be made in single-family homes, however. Nowadays investors must create their own property appreciation. Would you like to earn extra money by creating equity in homes that you can resell? The value you create by doing improvements can represent substantial profits. Feel free to revisit chapter 5 and use the steps described there to upgrade your single-family home. A little work can go a long way.

This chapter's methods for finding bargain-priced single-family homes and making improvements that can boost their value will provide you with a foundation from which to generate a substantial income. You can profit from fix-up work, and sweat equity pays big dividends. To create additional value, look for properties that are neglected and obviously need work. You want to find a single-family home and improve its physical condition, appeal, and livability.

When you run across a neglected, bargain-priced property or one that has been on the market for some time and it's likely the owner will accept a below-market proposal, use this checklist to help with your preliminary inspection of the house:

- To learn the worst, start in the basement or crawl space beneath the house; this is where you are most likely to see structural defects. Have the basement walls started to sag? Cracks or crumbling concrete are signs of dampness and weakness. If you see watermarks on the walls, you know the area has been flooded. Look for evidence of moisture. If a sump pump has been installed, you'll know there are flooding problems.
- You can make your own quick test for termites and dry rot. Take a screwdriver and probe the timbers (called *joists*) that support the floor above. Then probe the sills that run flat along the top of the foundation walls. Sometimes your screwdriver won't go in at all—a good sign. But sometimes it will crunch in easily and uncover bugs gnawing away at the wood.
- Ask for a termite clearance before you buy. Most termite and dry-rot damage can be repaired at nominal cost. Fear of termites creates bargains for people who know how to correct minor damage.
- In the basement or crawl space (if there is one), look further at the joists. They may be rotting from water that has seeped down from the kitchen or bathrooms. Check to see if any joists have pulled away from supporting sills or masonry. If so, this could mean the

foundation has shifted and the walls have moved, which could call for major rebuilding.

- Take a look at the water pipes. Galvanized pipes will probably need to be replaced with copper.

- Take a look at the electrical box. If it has only four or six circuits (which is typical in old houses), the house's electrical system is outdated. A house with eight to twelve rooms needs sixteen to twenty circuits and a circuit breaker panel. This helps with today's modern appliances and will also save you money on insurance.

- See if the chimney has separated. Look for missing mortar and broken bricks. A stair-step pattern of cracks in a brick wall is evidence of a major separation. This may indicate that repairs are needed as the house continues to shift its weight.

- Deterioration often begins in the outside windowsills and frames. Check for rot in these areas.

- Check the roof. Send up a professional roofer to get his opinion. Do the gutters show signs of leaks or breaks? If you can, go up to the attic and look around with a flashlight. If there are leaks, you will see telltale water stains.

- Inside the house, check for warped doors that will not close. Check also for creaky floors, loose tiling, inadequate plumbing, and other obvious flaws. Are there enough electrical outlets? Check the water heater, too; it should hold thirty or forty gallons of water.

- A bad floor plan can cut into a house's resale value. Appraisers have an eye for poor layout. Can you get from car to kitchen without walking all around the house? Can you go from bedroom to bathroom without being seen from the living areas? Today's designers say that two bathrooms are now the minimum, and one bathroom should adjoin the master bedroom.

These are all points to keep in mind. A few shortcomings do not necessarily mean that you should not buy, but they will be a warning that you should get an expert appraisal, as well as estimates to determine the cost of essential improvements.

Improving Your Property for Profit

Profitable improvements begin with a creative imagination. Appealing improvements add to a house's value. After you have focused on a specific neighborhood, try to obtain sales comparables in your area of interest. If a particular property sold for an above-average price, identify which of the property's features enabled the house to sell for more.

If and when you find a bargain-priced property, adapt those winning features into your improvement plans. If you are buying an older property (fifty to seventy years old), simply modernizing the property can result in good profits for you.

Developing a Profit Objective

After you set a realistic value for your upgraded property, add up your cost estimates. A realistic future value will help you figure out the most you could pay for a property while still making a profit.

Profits from doing improvements are viable even as the housing cycle struggles. The following is an actual case study from the past several years in the midst of the correcting housing market.

A couple purchases a three-bedroom, two-bath house in a California coastal area for $600,000. They had done their market research and determined that this negotiated price was about 20 percent under market, as the average sales comparisons in the neighborhood were in the $750,000 range. The house is located in an older neighborhood, and most of these comparables have been considerably updated. Some have sold for as high as $900,000 (thereby establishing the area's ceiling), but none has sold for less than $575,000. The house was built in 1946, along with the rest of the neighborhood. No parts of the structure have been changed except for some cosmetic updating to the bathrooms and kitchen. These improvements look to have been done in the 1970s. The foundation and crawl space under the house were inspected by a professional and determined to be in good condition with no shifting or dry rot. The buyers inspected the attic and found buckets strategically placed to catch any water leaks from the roof; they negotiated a credit for roof repair with the sellers.

The likely new owners projected that after completion of improvements they would create a house valued at about $900,000, based upon the neighborhood's comparable sales. Their personal objectives included maintaining a three-to-one return on the cost of improvements. In other words, their goal was to spend $100,000 on improvements to create an additional $300,000 in value (cost of house: $600,000; finished value: $900,000). They determined that the improvement budget for labor and materials should not exceed $100,000. Based on the renovations that this couple wants to do to the house, and in consideration of comparable neighborhood sales, it will be difficult to keep the budget under this projection. The new owners decide to invest considerable sweat equity to maintain their profit margins.

Renovations/Improvements

After close of escrow but before the new owners move in, the following renovations are completed:

- Reconditioning of walls and ceiling by applying a texturing compound
- Prime and finish painting of the interior
- Replacing existing baseboards throughout with tall, four-inch, up-to-date material
- Replacing the old electrical receptacles and light switches
- Replacing all ceiling light fixtures with new modern materials
- Sanding and refinishing the hardwood flooring throughout
- Applying an up-to-date stone material to the hearth and surrounding area of the fireplace in the living room

After completing these renovations, the new owners move in. The most expensive improvement they have contemplated so far is the addition of about 400 square feet as a family room. They determine that this will add the most to the improved value. These extensive renovations will nearly double the living area, excluding the bedrooms.

In order to get a city permit to do the addition, the owners will need to submit architectural plans. They begin interviewing several architects to get bids to do the drawings.

Since this will take some time to complete, in the meantime, the buyers begin replacing the old windows in the house one at a time. The new double-pane windows are quite an improvement on the old, leaky original windows.

The new owners purchased the materials—but not labor—to complete the above work. Their labor, in the form of sweat equity, contributed substantially to saving money on installation. They did most of the work in their spare time and with the help of instructional books they found at the local home improvement store.

The new owners do the demolition work on one of the bathrooms. They also retexture and paint the walls and ceiling. After removing the old fixtures from the bathroom, they hire a contractor to install the following:

- New bathtub and fixtures
- New pedestal sink and toilet
- New marble slab walls surrounding the bathtub
- New marble floor
- New medicine cabinet
- New glass bathtub doors

While the contractor works in the bathroom, the couple orders wooden shutters for their new window coverings throughout the home.

Upon completion of the architect's plans, the owners submit the package to the city building department for approval. The building department quickly approves the plans and grants the couple a building permit.

Many contractors are interviewed and subsequently bid on the job. The objective is to add 25 to 30 percent to the square footage of the house. This will represent the most valuable improvement thus far.

A contractor with a reasonable bid is selected; the owners feel confident that they can work with him.

His bid includes the following:

- Demolition and disposal of the old outdoor patio that is currently in the place where the new family room will be built
- Excavation and prepping of the area where the foundation will be constructed, plus the new foundation itself
- Framing of the new addition and demolition of existing exterior wall areas
- Installation of owner-bought doors and windows

The cost breakdown is below:

- Demolition and disposal $3,250
- Excavation $1,750
- Foundation $8,000
- Framing $15,000
Total Bid $28,000

The owners give a deposit to the contractor, and work begins. As work progresses the contractor suggests that he install an interior cathedral ceiling to make the room appear larger and generally more desirable. The owners agree, and the contractor prepares a change order. He draws up a plan and submits it for approval to the city as a modification. Basically it calls for a change from a flat roof to a hip roof design, which substantially improves the exterior appearance. The cost of this change is $13,250, which is added to the original bid.

After approximately three months, all of the planned work is completed to the owners' satisfaction. The house passes all city inspections with no problems.

The couple decides that since the new family room addition is connected to the kitchen, now is the best time to complete the kitchen remodel as well. The owners agree to give the work to their current contractor. The labor and materials will include the following:

- All the electrical work for the new addition and kitchen, $8,850 including new service upgrade

- New kitchen plumbing and installation of island for sink and countertop $2,616
- New fireplace framing and exterior stucco for family room $3,203
- Drywall and texturing for family room and kitchen (owners will apply prime and finish paint) $4,140
- Install owner-bought kitchen cabinets $1,250
- Install finish trim $1,320
- Install hardwood flooring (for family room and kitchen) $2,300

In addition to the above contracts for labor and materials, the owners have purchased the following items:

- New double-pane windows throughout, which includes new patio sliding door, large picture frame window, and French door for the addition (cost: $8,174)
- Custom wooden window shutters ($1,742)
- New custom kitchen cabinets installed by contractor as per agreement (cost of materials: $11,241)
- A granite fabricator contracted to provide material and labor for kitchen countertops and surrounding areas ($5,255)
- Architect's plans and city building permits ($3,278)
- Labor and finish materials for two bathrooms ($16,320)

The owners provided much of the labor to prep for the installation of the finish materials. Thus, the total cost of the remodeling project is $110,939—about $111,000, or 18 percent of the purchase price of the home.

Upon completion of the remodel and renovation it is apparent that the owners have added substantially to the value of the property. The question is by how much? They decide to get an up-to-date appraisal to obtain a new, postrenovation opinion of value.

Up-to-Date Appraisal/Finished Value

The appraiser's written report notes that the property features granite kitchen countertops and hardwood floors throughout, in addition to a remodeled kitchen and bathrooms, a new addition, new copper plumbing, and new windows. Based on comparable sales data, the appraiser determines the new value to be $840,000.

Let's analyze how this new value reflects on the cost of the improvements. With a purchase price of $600,0000 and an improvement expense of $111,000, we determine that the owners are "into" the property for $711,000.

The value of the property was improved by $240,000 with an expense of $111,000. This provides a gross profit ratio of a little greater than 2:0; the owners more than doubled their return based on the $111,000 improvement expense. Is this a good ratio? It certainly is acceptable considering that this was all done in a correcting real estate market. In an expanding housing and economic environment, a larger margin of say three dollars for every one dollar expended on improvements could be expected. Three to one certainly provides for a substantial margin of safety. But even with this current example, the return can be considered good, given the economic environment.

The costs of fix-up and purchase prices in your market area may differ from those discussed here, but the fundamentals and underlying principles are the same.

Financing for Improvements

You will need to use some imagination to find ways to finance improvements. At www.hud.gov you can find several methods for getting loans for improvements. One is the Section 203(k) Program, and another is Title I improvement loans.

The Federal Housing Administration (FHA), which is part of the Department of Housing and Urban Development (HUD), administers various single-family mortgage insurance programs. These programs operate through FHA-approved lending institutions, which submit applications to have properties appraised and have buyers' credit approved. These lenders fund mortgage loans, which the Department insures. (HUD does not make direct loans to help people buy homes.)

Section 203(k) Program

The *Section 203(k) Program* is the Department's primary program for the rehabilitation and repair of single-family properties. As such, it is an important tool for neighborhood revitalization and for expanding homeownership opportunities.

Most mortgage financing plans provide only permanent financing. That is, the lender will not usually close the loan and release the mortgage proceeds unless the condition and value of the property provide adequate loan security. When rehabilitation is involved, this means that a lender typically requires the improvements to be finished before a long-term mortgage is made.

When a home buyer wants to purchase a house in need of repair or modernization, the home buyer usually has to obtain interim financing first to purchase the house and additional interim financing to do the rehabilitation construction, and then, when the work is completed, a permanent mortgage to pay off the interim loans. Often the interim financing (the acquisition and construction loans) involves relatively high interest rates and short amortization periods. The Section 203(k) Program was designed to address this situation. The borrower can get just one mortgage loan, at a long-term fixed (or adjustable) rate, to finance both the acquisition and the rehabilitation of the property.

To provide funds for the rehabilitation of the property, the mortgage amount is based on the projected value of the property with the work completed and takes into account the cost of the work. To minimize the risk to the lender, the mortgage loan (the maximum allowable amount) is eligible for endorsement by HUD as soon as the mortgage proceeds are disbursed and a rehabilitation escrow account is established. At this point the lender has a fully insured mortgage loan.

This program can be used to accomplish rehabilitation and/or improvement of an existing one- to four-unit dwelling in one of three ways:

- To purchase a dwelling and the land on which the dwelling is located and rehabilitate it
- To purchase a dwelling on another site, move it onto a new foundation on the mortgaged property, and rehabilitate it
- To refinance existing liens secured against the subject property and rehabilitate the dwelling

Only first trust deeds and/or mortgages are eligible for funding.

Luxury items and improvements are not eligible as a cost rehabilitation. However, the homeowner can use the 203(k) program to finance painting and building room additions, decks, and other features even if the home does not need any other improvements.

If you have questions about the 203(k) program or are interested in getting a 203(k) insured mortgage loan, you should get in touch with an FHA-approved lender in your area.

Title I

Under *Title I*, HUD insures lenders against most losses on home improvement loans. Approved lending institutions use their own funds to make loans to eligible borrowers to finance home improvements. The Title I program insures loans to finance moderate rehabilitation of properties and may be used to insure such loans for up to twenty years on either single-family or multifamily properties. The maximum loan amount for improving a single-family home is $25,000.

FHA insures private lenders against the risk of default for up to 90 percent of any single loan. The annual premium for this insurance is $1 per $100 of the amount advanced, and it is sometimes covered by a higher interest rate.

Title I loans may be used to finance permanent property improvements that protect or improve the basic livability or utility of the property.

Applications must be submitted to a Title I–approved lender. The HUD website (www.hud.gov) offers a searchable list of approved lenders.

Bank Improvement Loans

Finally, a frequently used alternative for financing improvements is applying at the local bank where the investor already has an existing working relationship. Often, if you are seeking a loan of this kind, you will need to submit a before (or "as-is") appraisal and an "after completion of work" appraisal. Most appraisers can help with this. You must also submit to the bank the types of improvements you want to make and their costs. Usually, even if you plan to provide your own labor, you will need to provide a contractor's cost in your budget.

Chapter Recap

A single-family home is usually the first property bought by realty investors. As you search for deals that meet your criteria, keep these points in mind:

- Look for motivated sellers who are unable to repair their properties. Your objective should be to buy at least 20 percent under market value.
- Concentrate on property listings that have been on the market for a while.
- Focus on long-term owners who have not modernized or kept up their properties.
- Check "house for rent" ads for possible properties to buy.
- Search public notices for divorces, retirements, deaths, and foreclosures.
- Search for real estate owned (REO) by banks and other financial institutions. Work with brokers that specialize in foreclosures or short sales.
- Once you begin negotiating on a bargain property, study comparable sales and values so you can develop a plan to improve the property.
- Determine your improvement costs, the amount you can pay to purchase the property, and your expected profit. You can determine much of this from studying the comparable sales in the neighborhood you have chosen.

-9-

A Word on Taxes

If a man didn't make mistakes, he'd own the world in a month. But if he didn't profit by his mistakes, he wouldn't own a blessed thing.

—*Edwin Lefevre, statesman*

The only two constants in life are death and taxes. And as an income property owner, you'll find no truer words have been said. In many cases, income property owners pay more than their fair share of annual property taxes for schools and for city and county governments. Property owners also pay annual fees for business licenses in many cities, because after all, they are running businesses. Property taxes and local fees are each owner's responsibility even though such expenses can be passed on to tenants in the form of higher rents.

Despite these costs, however, there are also certain federal and state tax benefits that the income property owner should take advantage of. This helps balance the effect of paying a disproportionate share of local property taxes and fees. Few investments offer more tax advantages than real estate. This chapter will give you most of the basic information, but you should absolutely seek out more in-depth tax information from your accountant or tax preparer.

Depreciation

The IRS allows you to recover the cost of investment property through yearly tax deductions called the *depreciation expense*. Three basic factors determine how much depreciation you can deduct: (a) your basis (or cost including purchase price) in the property; (b) the recovery period for the property (this means the amount of years you have to write it off); and (c) the depreciation method used.

Depreciation means that a building loses some of its value each year. You can deduct depreciation only on the part of your property that is used for rental purposes. Depreciation reduces your basis, or cost, for figuring gain or loss on a later sale or exchange of the property. So taking depreciation deductions shrinks your cost basis, thereby increasing your gain on a sale. Before you plan a sale you need to figure this into your potential gain and realize how it will substantially increase profit—and in so doing, also increase your taxable liability.

However, during your ownership, utilizing the depreciation expense can reduce your taxable net operating income. By taking all the depreciation expenses that the law allows, the income property owner can increase net revenues by decreasing income taxes. In some cases the depreciation allowance can entirely offset in-pocket income.

The best time to set up depreciable accounts is when you first acquire a property. Loss from depreciation comes as a result of several factors, including weather damage, general wear and tear, and the newer features of more modern buildings. Tax laws allow you to expense the building, but not the land. Since you cannot depreciate the land, you should allocate as low a cost as possible for land and attribute the balance of your cost to the depreciable building value. To determine land and building values, consult local real estate brokers. You should also analyze recent property tax bills, since land and building values are often itemized. This is the most common method to determine the percentage of purchase price for land and building.

The cost basis, as the tax authorities like to call it, would include your actual purchase price, as well as all other costs involved in obtaining title. These expenses include the following:

- Abstract fees
- Legal fees
- Recording fees
- Surveys
- Transfer taxes
- Title insurance
- Any additional fees the seller owes that you agree to pay—such as back taxes or interest, recording or mortgage fees, charges for improvements or repairs, and sales commissions (These attribute to your overall out-of-pocket cost, or basis, on the property.)

You cannot include these settlement fees and closing costs in your basis in the property:

- Fire insurance premiums
- Rent or other charges relating to occupancy of the property before closing
- Charges connected with getting or refinancing loans, such as the following:
  - Points (loan origination fees)
  - Mortgage insurance premiums
  - Loan assumption fees
  - Cost of credit reports
  - Fees for lender-required appraisals

Also, do not include amounts placed in escrow for the future payment of expenses such as taxes and insurance.

Add to the cost of your property the amount that an addition or improvement actually cost you, including any amount you borrowed to make the addition or improvement. This includes all direct costs, such as material and paid labor, but not your own labor. It would also include all expenses related to the addition or improvement.

For example, if you had an architect draw up plans for remodeling your property, the architect's fee would be part of the cost of remodeling.

Or, if you had your lot surveyed to put up a fence, you should factor the cost of the survey into the cost of the fence.

At this time you can take a straight-line depreciation, writing the building off on a declining 27½-year schedule. On many apartment houses, you can depreciate 75 percent of the purchase price or cost as an annual write-off, which assumes a 25 percent allocation for land value.

Each year you can deduct 1/27.5 of its depreciable value from the income it produces before taxes. As previously mentioned, usually this loss of value is mostly imaginary, assuming the market value increases—but the deduction is real. When you prepare your income tax, you offset the imaginary loss against your actual profit.

Keep in mind that sooner or later you will need to reinvest in your property. Roof repairs or replacements and exterior paint will become necessary during your ownership. In this section, I'll use the example of the Rosewood Apartments (from chapter 6) to demonstrate how to make maximum use of the depreciation allowance.

The net income from the Rosewood is about $50,000 each year. The latest annual depreciation allowance was $15,457. Thus, the deduction shelters approximately 30 percent of the income. This deduction is calculated by dividing the cost (mostly the purchase price) by a declining 27½-year schedule.

On newer purchases this deduction can sometimes approach 100 percent of the building's net income. The longer you own and operate a property, the more likely it is that the building's income will increase. Eventually, your depreciation deduction becomes a smaller percentage of net income, so the deduction is more valuable in the early years of ownership.

When the depreciation deduction runs low, some investors take this as a signal to sell. They become motivated to start a new depreciation schedule on a new building solely for tax purposes.

What's most important is that you are cognizant that if you choose to sell depreciated property for a gain, the deductions you have taken will shrink your cost basis (the original purchase price). This will substantially increase your tax liability, especially if you have owned the property for many years.

Tax-Free Loan Proceeds

You can acquire more property by borrowing on property that you already own and using the tax-free loan proceeds to fund your investment. The loan has to be repaid, but you do not have to pay taxes for money you receive from refinancing.

Consider the Commodore Apartments from chapter 6. When it was determined that the equity in the property exceeded 50 percent of the value, we took out a loan of $575,000 to repay the existing loan of $303,000. Since the loan had to be repaid through liquidating payments, there were no taxes due on the proceeds obtained through refinancing.

Section 1031/Like-Kind Exchanges

Property is the most valuable asset that you can own. Property can also be sold and traded like a commodity. If you trade business or investment property solely for the same kind of property—which you will continue to hold as business or investment property—you can postpone reporting gains. These trades are known as *section 1031* or *like-kind exchanges*. It is as if the property you receive in a like-kind exchange were a continuation of the property you gave up, so this is looked at as a continuation of ownership.

You do not have to report any part of your gain if you receive only like-kind property. But if you also receive money or other property (boot) in the exchange, you must report your gain to the extent of the money and the fair market value of the other property received.

If you acquire property in a like-kind exchange, the cost basis of that property is generally the same as the cost basis of the property you transferred. If, for example, you exchange a real estate investment with an adjusted cost basis of $100,000 for some other real estate investment, the basis of your new property is the same as the basis of the old property ($100,000). However, if in addition to giving up like-kind property, you pay money in a like-kind exchange, you still have no recognized gain or loss. The cost basis of the property received is the cost basis of the property given up plus the money paid.

With a deferred exchange, you can postpone your gain. In this type of exchange, you transfer property that you use in business or hold for investment, and later you receive like-kind property that you will use in business or hold for investment. The property you receive is replacement property. The transaction must be an exchange (property for property); the original property cannot be exchanged for money that is then used to buy replacement property.

The replacement property will not be treated as like-kind property unless certain identification and receipt requirements are met:

- You must not receive actual or constructive receipt of money or unlike property for less than full consideration for the property you transfer.
- You must identify the property to be received within forty-five days after the date you transfer the property given up in the exchange.
- The property must be received by the earlier of the following dates:
    a. The 180th day after the date on which you transfer the property given up in the exchange.
    b. The due date, including extensions, for your tax return for the tax year in which the transfer of the property given up occurs.

As you can see, strict rules govern these exchanges, whether you are trading up or down. The good news is that there are many small firms that can help you with the rules and the escrows involved in these transactions.

As an income property owner, you can use the benefits of an IRS 1031 exchange to reduce turnover profits when expanding your property holdings. The only drawback seems to be the fact that you must continue with your smaller cost basis when trading up. This will seriously reduce depreciation allowances to shelter operating net income on your traded-up property.

In some cases it may be advantageous to sell outright and pay the capital gain tax, and then buy a larger property and get the stepped-up basis for depreciation purposes. When the occasion calls for it, your accountant may advise selling, instead of trading. This decision will depend on your gain and how much depreciation you have taken.

My purpose in including this chapter is to make you aware of the tax benefits available to income property owners. In this book I would not attempt an analysis of income taxes. What I have described are simply some basic tax benefits that you should be aware of. Before completing a transaction that appears complex from a tax angle, you should consult an attorney or accountant with expertise in real estate tax matters.

Chapter Recap

Property owners can use a number of different methods to reduce what they pay in taxes. Here are the most common:

- The annual depreciation deduction, which allows you to save taxes on your operating income
- Tax-free loan proceeds, which are nontaxable funds you get through refinancing
- Like-kind exchanges (also called 1031 exchanges), which allow you to postpone your gains when you exchange properties

-10-

Estate Planning and Other Things to Consider

Success is to be measured not so much by the position that one has reached in life as by the obstacles which he has overcome.

—*Booker T. Washington, educator*

Protecting Your Assets

I hope that by this point this book has helped you amass the knowledge required to build a hefty investment property portfolio. Once acquired, these assets will make up your overall financial present and future, but what happens after that? Protecting your assets should be a major consideration in estate planning. As you increase your long-term holdings, like apartment buildings and other income property, you need to protect your equity from potential liabilities.

Since I do not advocate selling your buildings, I recommend that you develop entities that can hold title to your properties for the long term. These entities will offer you protection from potential issues down the road. The longer you hold your properties, the more likely it is that you will be exposed to things such as liability lawsuits. During your holding period, you are likely to build up large amounts of equity from improvements to the property's net income, inflation, and the natural paydown of the principal on your mortgages. You need to do all you can to limit the damaging effects of a lawsuit on the equity that you have worked so hard to build up.

Millions of lawsuits are filed in America every year. We live in the age of litigation. We have an unfortunate combination of bold lawyers and a huge difference of wealth in this country.

A fast-growing segment of litigation deals with "premises liability" lawsuits. The fact is, if you own real estate, you are a sitting duck for lawsuits. You can be sued by a tenant, by the guest of a tenant, or by a contractor working on your property. A suit could arise from something as simple as a slip and fall, or something a lot worse, such as a structural defect, like a leaky roof or faulty plumbing, that causes damage to a tenant's property—or even worse, causes your structure to collapse and cause a wrongful death. Unfortunately, while real estate has the potential to generate wealth, it also has the potential to generate liability.

You should be aware that, to an extent, you *can* protect yourself from the liability that you generate. How you hold property can make a big difference in how much damage can be done.

You can take title to real estate in many different ways. Almost all people hold real estate investments personally, as individual owners or as married couples, in their own names—such as husband and wife, as joint tenants. This is the easiest way to own property. The other choice is to own the property in some type of entity. An entity has a legal identity, separate from its owners, and can own property.

You should discuss with your attorney the entity that might best serve your needs. Examples include corporations, limited partnerships, limited liability companies (LLCs), and trusts.

Let us assume for the moment that someone slipped and fell on your property and severely injured himself or herself. If a lawyer can show that you knew about the faulty step or loose handrail that contributed to the accident, he will say that you allowed a dangerous condition to exist on your property. If that same lawyer finds a significant amount of equity or assets in your name, then he will more easily be able to recover damages if he wins the lawsuit. The lawyer would prefer to have a sufficient insurance policy to go after, but if the damages are high enough, he will aim for your equity in the property or even your other assets. If the injured person's lawyer discovers that you own a couple of rental properties in which you have equity, he will become more inclined to pursue the suit. Often, these assets are all in the owner's name and are easily identifiable. All of these assets could be at risk in a lawsuit, so you must take steps to protect them.

Your lawyer can help you put an asset protection plan in place. Despite the fact that you have multiple assets, you could have arranged to put the property where the slip and fall occurred, for example, into a separate entity. This means the liability cannot get back to the owner. The only asset the plaintiff's lawyer can go after is the equity of the property where the event occurred. If there is very little equity in the property, it will reduce the lawyer's aggressiveness. Similarly, if you have a large equity in the property where the event happened, there will be nothing you can do about it. You will not be able to prevent the tenant from seeking liability from the insurance company, and if there is not enough insurance coverage, going after the property. But you can stop the liability from threatening *all* of your assets.

Since my holdings are in an LLC (limited liability company), I am more familiar with ways that this entity can protect you. Putting each of your properties into a separate LLC is expensive. But if you do so, the liability generated by each property will be limited to that property and will not threaten your other assets. In other words, each individual asset will be protected from all of the others. Since it is cumbersome to have an LLC for each property, you may choose to operate, say, two LLCs. In one LLC you may put your riskier properties, and in the other, your less risky assets. Similarly, if you have substantial equity in a property, you may not want to mix it with other high-risk, high-liability properties.

It is important to know that there are ways to protect your equity. But, since asset protection can become complex, you need your attorney to advise you on the best course of action to suit your needs.

Asset protection and the manner in which you hold title to your income properties form one line of defense against lawsuits; another mode of protection is the insurance that you carry on your buildings. The amount of insurance you buy is up to you, but you should get as much as you need to be able to sleep comfortably. The factors to consider are the size of the property, the likelihood of a liability-generating event, and the likelihood of more than one liability-generating event in a year. I consider a liability policy of $2,000,000 per property in the five-to-twenty-unit range to be adequate. You can then back up these liability amounts with an umbrella policy that would offer additional protection in the event that you exhaust your individual policy amounts. Umbrella policies are inexpensive and very worthwhile. Your insurance agent can provide you with more information on this type of policy.

Your first line of defense against lawsuits, however, is maintaining your properties in tip-top condition. If you stay on top of all maintenance and upkeep, you can prevent a good majority of these types of lawsuits. As I have stressed repeatedly, it is essential that improvements and maintenance be the focus of your operation. This will not only enable you to obtain better-paying tenants, it will also maximize your net operating income. I would go so far as to say that if you cannot make this your first priority in operating real estate, then you should not buy income property. Too many investors have lost their down payments due to lawsuits and local municipal authorities closing their properties due to inadequate maintenance and repairs.

Habitability Issues

Below is a list of some liability-generating issues you must pay particular attention to and contend with.

- *Heat.* Every apartment must have a working, built-in heater. This does not include a plug-in electric heater. Without a heater, the unit cannot be considered an apartment.
- *Leaky roofs and plumbing.* You must maintain your building so that it is watertight. No water leaks from either the roof or any of the plumbing is permissible. Many owners have gotten into trouble because of leaky roofs and plumbing, so be certain your properties allow for no water intrusion. You must maintain an operating reserve fund so you can replace worn-out roofs and repair all plumbing leaks, as they occur.

- *Extermination.* You must keep your properties free of all rodents and insects. A local pest control company can handle this for you, and it is a very small maintenance expense. Encourage your tenants to keep good housekeeping standards to minimize the problem. Your municipal authorities can help solve unusual problems in this area. For example, I once had a pregnant raccoon take up residence in a roof attic above four apartments. The city inspector told me that there was nothing I could do about it until she had her babies. When this happens, the raccoon would leave on her own, along with her new family. The raccoon had entered through a broken rooftop vent, so tip-top maintenance could have eliminated this problem before it even began. At another time, in a fourteen-unit property, a number of pigeons began gathering every day at the top of a stairwell. Needless to say, this created quite a health hazard. After experimenting with several attempts to eliminate the problem, I discovered that a tenant was feeding the pigeons on a daily basis. I eventually had to speak to the tenant to solve the pigeon problem.

- *Garbage.* You are responsible for maintaining adequate garbage receptacles for your buildings. This means your containers must be of adequate size and capacity to handle the garbage generated by your occupants. This can vary depending on the number of people living in your units. This can also vary depending on whether the building is normally completely rented, or if there are consistent vacancies.

  In addition, you must ensure that your property is free of debris, old tenant furniture, and nonoperating vehicles. Someone (maybe your general manager) must be responsible for picking up old tenant belongings and items of furniture and hauling them to the dump on a consistent basis. Some municipalities operate a vehicle abatement unit that tows cars from private property. Look into whether your city has such a department. Normally the service is free of charge and will tow cars from your property as directed.

- *Illegal drugs.* If you allow any illegal drug activity to occur on your property, you risk having the local municipal authorities close down your building for as long as one year. You could also be subject to a fine. The illegal activity could take place in a particular tenant's apartment or even in the common areas of your property. Either way, you need to eradicate the problem. In addition, you risk having the good tenants in your building move or even withhold their rent, if you allow this nuisance to continue.

  For your own safety, you should contact your local police to help you with a problem of this nature. Sometimes they can provide evidence (if they make an arrest, for example) that you can use in an eviction. More than likely, though, you will need to evict the tenant for another reason; use or sale of drugs is hard to prove.

  To expedite the process, you may offer the tenant cash to move. Whatever you do, you need to act fast before it becomes a widespread neighborhood problem.

- *Handrails and stairs.* Other sources of problems are faulty steps and loose handrails. Tenants slip and fall all the time. If you permit a dangerous situation to exist, you could be exposed to a claim from a tenant or a tenant's guest. You need to be vigilant regarding the maintenance of these items. If you rebuild any exterior steps, get a permit for them and have them inspected by the city upon completion to be sure they meet local building codes. Later, if you have an accident on your new stairs, you can bet that somebody will check to see if your stairs were rebuilt with a permit.

These are but a few issues that you can and very likely will be faced with as an investment property owner. If you pay attention to the habitability issues listed above, you will have very few problems with your tenants.

To review, you need to maintain certain defenses to protect the equities you will establish:

- Keep extremely well maintained and modernized apartments.
- Be cautious in selecting tenants for your vacancies.

- Maintain insurance liability policies of about $2,000,000 per property. Take out an umbrella policy after consulting with your insurance agent.
- Hold title to your investment property in an entity that is consistent with the advice of your attorney. For example, if you have multiple properties, you might consider maintaining two LLCs after discussing with your attorney which properties should go into which LLC.

Above all, give good value to the people who rent from you. Good management is the key to any successful enterprise. Value is hard to define, but renters can sense its existence. If they are satisfied, they will continue to rent from you, and they will recommend you to others. If you steadfastly adhere to the above guidelines, you will have very few tenant problems.

Business Structure

As you accumulate rental properties, your management duties will be much easier if the rentals are located in close proximity to one another. Rent collections, repairs, and ongoing maintenance will all be easier to handle. Try to specialize in one area or neighborhood of your city.

If possible, avoid accumulating a collection small buildings. Management of most buildings that are not large enough to justify a resident manager will consume more of your time over the long run. So start looking for larger buildings of at least ten units each or, preferably, more. If your market area is more rural than urban, you might try to assemble duplexes, single-family homes, and three- and four-unit buildings that are at least in close proximity to each other.

Once you have accumulated substantial capital or investment equity, it is important not to put all that you have into one property. By dividing your funds over two or more properties, you will have more flexibility. Also, if one investment turns out to be a bomb or less profitable than you expected, you should have other resources you can draw on in order to keep moving forward.

By making many offers on income properties and adhering to the fundamental of making only small down payments, you can acquire a large amount of property in a short time. The question will not be whether you can purchase enough property, but which properties you should purchase. The properties must be serviced, managed, and properly cared for. There will come a time when you need to hire someone to handle the detailed management of your property. You will have to decide whether or not you want to expand to the extent that you are able to hire someone to handle the day-to-day management. Your answer will depend on your ultimate goal. Do you want to continue to expand and grow in the real estate investment field indefinitely, or do you just want to grow to the point at which you have sufficient income?

At any rate, when you accumulate forty to fifty units, you may explore the possibility of hiring a general manager. By this time, you should have adequate net income to pay your manager a salary (and be sure to withhold employment taxes!). In addition to other duties, your manager could modernize your apartments as described in chapter 5. To an extent, this will relieve you from the day-to-day management chores. You might also consider hiring a part-time bookkeeper to handle the bill paying, but I would suggest that you reserve the duty of signing the checks yourself.

Hiring a general manager and a bookkeeper, as opposed to hiring a property management firm, can allow you to have more control of your business. If you do hire a property management company, you can expect to have higher vacancy and maintenance expenses. Because of their other responsibilities, you cannot expect them to devote the same level of attention to your properties that you would.

You could employ a variation of the above after you expand your holdings. For example, on your new acquisitions, you could utilize the general manager structure to bring your building up to date, fill the vacancies, and institute your own management style. Once your new building is running smoothly, you could turn it over to a property management firm and then move on to your next acquisition.

The possibilities are limitless, but the main thing to know is that apartment buildings need management. They are much more management intensive than, say, commercial properties or single-family homes.

Another point to remember is that you must always keep enough cash in reserve. Do not risk being trapped in the position of having borrowed recently, only to find that you are running out of cash again. You can probably project your cash position accurately most of the time, but unexpected events can throw a forecast badly out of line. Your water heater may spring a leak, or you may need to replace a worn-out roof. An unexpected layoff by a big employer in your area may leave many of your residents unable to pay their rent. Anything can and will happen.

How much reserve is enough? As a rule of thumb, one-and-a-half times your monthly gross scheduled rent is generally safe. That is, if you are prepared to ride out a six-week period when your rental income is totally used up by expenses, you can sleep soundly. So when you take out a loan, try to get one that is big enough to allow for this margin of safety.

You can line up additional temporary protection by opening an overdraft protection or guaranteed reserve account at one of your banks. A guaranteed reserve account is a checking account in which you can overdraw up to a specified amount without checks bouncing. It is another way of borrowing. The interest on your overdrafts will probably be the bank's prime rate plus a 5 or 6 percent margin. You will have a source of ready cash, without even asking for it. Just be sure to keep this privilege intact until the emergency arises. Do not overdraw for anything other than a real crisis.

Caution

It is the very fact that large quantities of real estate can be acquired so easily that leads me to offer this note of caution. Because it is so easy to control vast empires by applying the principles of pyramiding, some property owners proceed with such reckless abandon that they lose sight of whether they actually own any of the wealth they are controlling. The result is that they sometimes gain control over staggering quantities of real estate, while their actual equity in those holdings is negligible. They borrow to cover the debt service and other operating expenses. They elevate their standard of living far beyond what their real incomes warrant, and somewhere up there, they get caught in a bind, which can be devastating. As long as the real estate market has good financing, they may be able to prosper. Considerable inflation in real estate prices will also bail them out, due to the extra-large leverage positions they maintain.

Empire builders want to be the biggest in their particular cities. Many years ago, the famous William Zeckendorf was one of these people. He actually did assemble the world's biggest real estate empire. However, his dreams outran his resources. From the start of his career, Zeckendorf had been able to use his deal-making skills to acquire projects for which he lacked the funds, but in time, the underfunding caught up with him. In 1965, Zeckendorf found himself unable to make mortgage payments on his overextended empire that forced his company into bankruptcy.

In more recent times, due to the growth of realty syndicates and investment trusts, it has become rare to see any large, individual realty owners or developers in the news. But smaller, more typical empire builders can be found in every city. They buy too many properties, or a single property that is too big, and cannot pay enough attention to management of the property or properties. Mismanaged properties soon lose money. But these empire builders seldom notice because they are concentrating on acquiring bigger and better properties.

Another type of property owner wants to be worshipped as the richest man in town. He spends his capital gains—and even his cash flow—on flashy cars and other highly visible luxuries. To get more and more spendable cash, he borrows too heavily or invests too little in the upkeep of his properties (or both) and gets caught in a liquidity squeeze.

I have known several real estate operators who fit the above descriptions. They were very successful and bought very large, expensive mansions in the most prestigious neighborhoods of their cities. Suddenly, when financing for real estate dried up, as it does in every economic recession, they lost almost all of their holdings. They were young enough that they could have started over, but their confidence was so shattered that ultimately they could not begin again.

It should be fairly obvious that if you acquire vast quantities of property on a minimum budget, without regard to whether the investments will pay for themselves, you jeopardize your financial well-being. If you continue this type of operation for an extended period, you are going to run into trouble.

So I must caution you that, while leverage and pyramiding are the tools for getting ahead in real estate, I do not advocate the reckless pursuit of riches. You should be able to reach any reasonable goal within ten years, while employing sound real estate investment practices.

It is not realistic to expect to purchase a property for a small down payment, do zero improvements to increase the income, and still meet large balloon payment notes a few years down the road.

Stay realistic and keep in touch with the here and now. And you can always refer back to this book if you need advice.

On Buying/Selling

By the time you have acquired a couple of properties and made improvements, you will have learned a lot about financing. Sometimes it is a great advantage to refinance a property and keep it rather than selling it.

In many cases you will be able to refinance a property and receive nearly the same amount of cash from the refinance as what you would have realized from the sale of the property. That is possible because in refinancing there are no real estate commissions or other selling expenses, and there are no second notes to be carried back for the buyers. Often, as I have, you will be able to refinance properties for more than you paid for them, after completing renovations. You should figure the cost of refinancing to determine the funds you would realize, taking into consideration the capital gains tax payment that would be due if you decided to sell the property instead.

Don't forget to factor in the depreciation you have taken as gain for tax purposes. If the difference in cash to be realized is small, and particularly if selling would require carryback secondary financing, then you should consider whether it would be better to refinance and keep the property. If the property in question will generate cash flow after refinancing, will build up equity, and will probably increase in value, it is likely that selling will serve no useful purpose. All it would do is relieve you of the management responsibility. If the property is relatively trouble free and is in an area where property values are expected to hold up or even grow, then it may very well be to your advantage to hold the property for some time.

Too often, investors sell property just because they see a huge gain, but the costs of buying and selling can eat up too much of the profit. At the same time, the investor is deprived of the advantage of building up equity through holding the property over time, and the advantage of the tax savings that holding the property could afford. Instead of requiring that you pay out a portion of the gain in taxes, the property will usually produce a tax savings if it is held. When the value of the equity buildup and appreciation prospects are added to the tax savings that the property can produce, you may be able to see the advantages of holding it. But even so, try to acquire larger properties as you progress, so you can avoid getting bogged down with management chores.

If you do decide to sell, do so during a seller's market when (usually) there are more buyers chasing fewer properties. This alone can increase your selling price by as much as 20 percent—unlike when you are selling in a buyer's market.

In any long-term investment plan, your objective should be to create annuities with income property. You can create a cash flow that pays your bills, and you can build up a significant net worth through appreciation and principal paydowns on your mortgage loans. By continuously holding your properties, you are able to take advantage of certain periods when rents jump substantially. Due to market conditions, large rent increases occur over a couple of years and then stay flat for long periods of time. You want to be an owner when these periods of rental increase are of great benefit to you. Remember, your number-one objective is to create a crop that you can harvest twelve times a year (whether you are there or not).

Earlier in my career, I made over a million dollars buying and selling properties. Although it made for a good living, it did not build investment income or personal net worth. I eventually adopted the plan set forth in chapter 6, and it has created both a lifetime income and equity buildup. Don't get me wrong—it's okay to buy and sell, provided that you invest the profits in rent-producing property that you can keep long term.

In Conclusion

Congratulations on getting this far on the heavy subject of real estate investment. Your tenacity shows courage and persistence, two qualities that are essential for real estate success.

The fundamentals in these pages have worked for me. I hope you will find them of some benefit to you. I trust these strategies will assist you in making your real estate experiences fulfilling and profitable. May good fortune, great planning, and a little luck shine on you.

Chapter Recap

As a long-term real estate owner, you will need to concern yourself with a few key points:

- Protecting your assets by paying attention to the manner in which you hold title to the property
- Habitability issues that help avoid lawsuits
- Thinking about a business structure that works to your benefit as you expand your holdings
- Avoiding overexpansion, which can be dangerous to your financial well-being
- Choosing not to sell your property when you simply want to cash in on a quick gain
- Recognizing that real estate investing is a marathon, not a sprint

Appendix A

═══════════

Amortization Chart

How to Calculate Your Monthly Mortgage Payment Using a Factor Chart

Use this chart to figure out a monthly payment for *each* $1,000 borrowed over the time period desired. Find the payment factor at the intersection of the interest rate and the loan term (in years). Multiply the payment factor by the loan amount and then divide by 1000; this will give you the new monthly amortized payment for the loan. *Amortization payment factors are for reference only.* Some rates may be rounded or may contain typographical errors. Accuracy is not guaranteed.

Rate	Interest Only	10-Year	15-Year	20-Year	25-Year	30-Year
1.000	**0.08333**	**8.76041**	**5.98495**	**4.59894**	**3.76872**	**3.21640**
1.125	0.09375	8.81477	6.04008	4.65492	3.82558	3.27413
1.250	0.10417	8.86935	6.09554	4.71134	3.88297	3.33252
1.375	0.11458	8.92414	6.15132	4.76818	3.94090	3.39154
1.500	0.12500	8.97915	6.20743	4.82545	3.99936	3.45120
1.625	0.13542	9.03437	6.26386	4.88316	4.05836	3.51150
1.750	0.14583	9.08982	6.32061	4.94129	4.11789	3.57243
1.875	0.15625	9.14547	6.37769	4.99985	4.17795	3.63400
2.000	**0.16667**	**9.20135**	**6.43509**	**5.05883**	**4.23854**	**3.69619**
2.125	0.17708	9.25743	6.49281	5.11825	4.29966	3.75902
2.250	0.18750	9.31374	6.55085	5.17808	4.36131	3.82246

197

Rate	Interest Only	10-Year	15-Year	20-Year	25-Year	30-Year
2.375	0.19792	9.37026	6.60921	5.23834	4.42348	3.88653
2.500	0.20833	9.42699	6.66789	5.29903	4.48617	3.95121
2.625	0.21875	9.48394	6.72689	5.36014	4.54938	4.01651
2.750	0.22917	9.54110	6.78622	5.42166	4.61311	4.08241
2.875	0.23958	9.59848	6.84586	5.48361	4.67735	4.14892
3.000	**0.25000**	**9.65607**	**6.90582**	**5.54598**	**4.74211**	**4.21604**
3.125	0.26042	9.71388	6.96609	5.60876	4.80738	4.28375
3.250	0.27083	9.77190	7.02669	5.67196	4.87316	4.35206
3.375	0.28125	9.38014	7.08760	5.73557	4.93945	4.42096
3.500	0.29167	9.88859	7.14883	5.79960	5.00624	4.49045
3.625	0.30208	9.94725	7.21037	5.86404	5.07352	4.56051
3.750	0.31250	10.00612	7.27222	5.92888	5.14131	4.63116
3.875	0.32292	10.06521	7.33440	5.99414	5.20959	4.70237
4.000	**0.33333**	**10.12451**	**7.39688**	**6.05980**	**5.27837**	**4.77415**
4.125	0.34375	10.18403	7.45968	6.12587	5.34763	4.84650
4.250	0.35417	10.24375	7.52278	6.19234	5.41738	4.91940
4.375	0.36458	10.30369	7.58620	6.25922	5.48761	4.99285
4.500	0.37500	10.36384	7.64993	6.32649	5.55832	5.06685
4.625	0.38542	10.42420	7.71397	6.39417	5.62951	5.14140
4.750	0.39583	10.48477	7.77832	6.46224	5.70117	5.41647
4.875	0.40625	10.54556	7.84297	6.53070	5.77330	5.29208
5.000	**0.41667**	**10.60655**	**7.90794**	**6.59956**	**5.84590**	**5.36822**
5.125	0.42708	10.66776	7.97320	6.66881	5.91896	5.44487
5.250	0.43750	10.72917	8.03878	6.73844	5.99248	5.52204
5.375	0.44792	10.79079	8.10465	6.80847	6.06645	5.59971
5.500	0.45833	10.85263	8.17083	6.87887	6.14087	5.67789
5.625	0.46875	10.91467	8.23732	6.94966	6.21575	5.75656
5.750	0.47917	10.97692	8.30410	7.02084	6.29106	5.83573
5.875	0.48958	11.03938	8.37118	7.09238	6.36682	5.91538
6.000	**0.50000**	**11.10205**	**8.43857**	**7.16431**	**6.44301**	**5.99551**
6.125	0.51042	11.16493	8.50625	7.23661	6.51964	6.07611
6.250	0.52083	11.22801	8.57423	7.30928	6.59669	6.15717

Rate	Interest Only	10-Year	15-Year	20-Year	25-Year	30-Year
6.375	0.53125	11.29130	8.64250	7.38232	6.67417	6.23870
6.500	0.54167	11.35480	8.71107	7.45573	6.75207	6.32068
6.625	0.55208	11.41850	8.77994	7.52950	6.83039	6.40311
6.750	0.56250	11.48241	8.84909	7.60364	6.90912	6.48598
6.875	0.57292	11.54653	8.91854	7.67814	6.98825	6.56929
7.000	**0.58333**	**11.61085**	**8.98828**	**7.75299**	**7.06779**	**6.65302**
7.125	0.59375	11.67537	9.05831	7.82820	7.14773	6.73719
7.250	0.60417	11.74010	9.12863	7.90376	7.22807	6.82176
7.375	0.61458	11.80504	9.19923	7.97967	7.30880	6.90675
7.500	0.06250	11.87017	9.27101	8.05593	7.38991	6.99215
7.625	0.63542	11.93552	9.34130	8.13254	7.47141	7.07794
7.750	0.64583	12.00106	9.41276	8.20949	7.55329	7.16412
7.850	0.65625	12.06681	9.48450	8.28677	7.63554	7.25069
8.000	**0.66667**	**12.13276**	**9.55652**	**8.36440**	**7.71816**	**7.33765**
8.125	0.67708	12.19891	9.62882	8.44236	7.80115	7.42497
8.250	0.68750	12.26526	9.70140	8.52066	7.88450	7.51267
8.375	0.69792	12.33182	9.77426	8.59928	7.96821	7.60072
8.500	0.70833	12.39857	9.84740	8.67823	8.05227	7.68913
8.625	0.71875	12.46552	9.92080	8.75751	8.13668	7.77790
8.750	0.72917	12.53268	9.99449	8.83711	8.22144	7.86700
8.875	0.73958	12.60003	10.06844	8.91702	8.30653	7.95645
9.000	**0.75000**	**12.66758**	**10.14267**	**8.99726**	**8.39196**	**8.04623**
9.125	0.76042	12.73533	10.21716	9.07781	8.47773	8.13633
9.250	0.77083	12.80327	10.29192	9.15867	8.56382	8.22675
9.375	0.78125	12.87142	10.36695	9.23984	8.65023	8.31749
9.500	0.79167	12.93976	10.44225	9.32131	8.73697	8.40854
9.625	0.80208	13.00829	10.51781	9.40309	8.82402	8.49989
9.750	0.81250	13.07702	10.59363	9.48517	8.91137	8.59154
9.875	0.82292	13.14595	10.66971	9.56754	8.99904	8.68349
10.000	**0.83333**	**13.21507**	**10.74605**	**9.65022**	**9.08701**	**8.77572**

Appendix B

═══════

Land Contract – Sample Form

This Agreement is made and entered into by and between:

_____

(seller)

whose address is:

_____

hereinafter called Vendor and

_____

(buyer)

Whose address is:

_____

hereinafter called Vendee.

Witnesseth: The Vendor, for himself, his heirs and assigns, does hereby agree to sell to the Vendee, their heirs and assigns, the following real estate commonly known as:

_____

and further described; as:

together with all appurtenances, rights, privileges and easements and all buildings and fixtures in their present condition located upon said property.

1. CONTRACT PRICE. METHOD PAYMENT, INTEREST RATE:

In consideration whereof, the Vendee agrees to purchase the above described property for the sum of

_____ Dollars
($_____), payable as follows:

The sum of $_____ as down payment at the time of the execution of the within Land Contract the receipt of which is hereby acknowledged, leaving principal balance owed by Vendee of $_____ together with interest on the unpaid balance payable in consecutive monthly installments of $_____ beginning on the _____ day of _____, 20_____, and on the _____ day of each and every month thereafter until said balance and interest is paid in full, or until the _____ day of _____ 20_____ at which time the entire remaining balance plus accrued interest shall become due and payable. The Interest on the unpaid balance due hereon shall be _____ (_____%) per annum computed monthly, in accordance with a monthly amortization schedule during the life of this Contract.

Payments shall be made to the Vendor at the location above, unless otherwise directed by the Vendor, and such payments shall be credited first to the Interest, and the remainder to the principal or other sums due. The total amount of this obligation, both principal and interest, unpaid after making any such application of payments as herein receipted shall be the interest-bearing principal amount of this obligation for the next succeeding interest computation period. If any payment is not received within _____ (_____) days of payment date, there shall be a late charge of _____ (_____%) percent assessed. The Vendee may pay their entire balance due under this contract without payment penalty.

2. ENCUMBRANCES:

Said real estate is presently subject to a mortgage, and neither Vendor nor Vendee shall place any mortgage on the premises in excess of this Land Contract balance without prior written consent of the other party.

3. REAL ESTATE TAXES:

Real estate taxes shall be the responsibility of the Vendee as of the date of the execution of this agreement. Said taxes shall be escrowed and added to the principal and interest payment required hereunder.

4. INSURANCE AND MAINTENANCE:

The Vendor agrees to keep the premises insured against fire and other hazard for at least _____ Dollars ($_____), and shall escrow and add the cost for said insurance premiums to the Vendee's principal and interest obligation herein.

Vendor herein shall have the right to enter the premises at least once per year with twenty-four hours' notice to Vendee of his interest to exercise his right.

Vendee shall keep the building in a good state of repair and well painted at the Vendee expense and no additions or altercations shall be made to the building without the Vendor's permission, which shall not be unreasonably withheld. At such time as the Vendor inspects the premises and finds that repairs are necessary, Vendor shall request that these repairs be made within thirty (30) days at the Vendee's expense.

The Vendee has inspected the premises constituting the subject matter of this Land Contract, and no representations have been made to the Vendee by the Vendor in regard to the condition of said premises; and it is agreed that the said premises are being sold to the Vendee as the same now exits and that the Vendor shall have no obligation to do or furnish anything toward improvement of said premises, except as may be provided herein.

5. POSSESSION:

The Vendee shall be given possession of the above described premises upon Contract execution, or as otherwise provided herein and shall thereafter have and hold the same subject to the provisions for default hereinafter set forth.

6. ASSIGNMENT:

The Vendee shall not sell, assign, or pledge their interest in this Land Contract without the Vendor's written consent which consent shall not be unreasonably withheld.

7. DELIVERY OF DEED:

Upon full payment of this contract, the Vendee shall receive a General Warranty deed to the property free of all encumbrances except otherwise set forth.

8. DEFAULT:

If any installment payment to be made by the Vendee under the terms of this Land Contract is not paid by the Vendee when due or within one (1) Installment thereafter, the entire unpaid balance shall become due and collectable at the election of the

Vendor and the Vendor shall be entitled to all the remedies provided for by the laws of this state and/or to do any other remedies and/or relief now or hereafter provided for by law to such Vendor; and in the event of the breach of this contract in any other respect by the Vendee. Vendor shall be entitled to all relief now or hereinafter provided for by the laws of this state.

Failure of the Vendee to maintain current the status of all real estate taxes and insurance escrow payments and/or premiums as required herein shall permit Vendor the option to pay any such escrow amounts, premiums, taxes, interest, and/or penalty(ies), and to add same to the next due installment payment or principal amount owing under this contract, or to exercise any remedies available to Vendor.

Waiver by the Vendor of a default or a number of defaults in the performance hereof by the Vendee shall not be construed as a waiver of any default, no matter how similar.

In the event that the Vendor's interests in the property should become compromised or otherwise extinguished for any reason, or should there be an acceleration of any debt secured by the property, the Vendee shall be entitled to a refund of all down payment monies paid to the Vendor, plus the principal portion of any payments made to date, as follows: Upon notification of such conditions, Vendee agrees to suspend subsequent payments due hereunder, and must continue to occupy the property until required to vacate by judicial order. Vendee further agrees that any refund amounts due hereunder will be reduced by the amount of the missed payments. Both parties agree that this shall constitute the entire liability of the Vendor, and that Vendor shall have no liability to Vendee beyond this amount for any reason whatsoever.

9. GENERAL PROVISIONS:

There are no known pending orders issued by any governmental authority with respect to this property other than those spelled out herein prior to closing date for execution of this agreement.

It is agreed that this Land Contract shall be binding upon each of the parties, their administrators, executors, legal representatives, heirs and assigns.

10. SPECIAL PROVISIONS:

_____

_____

_____

_____

IN WITNESS WHEREOF, the parties hereby set their hands this _____ day of _____ 20_____,

WITNESS: _____

_____

VENDOR: _____

_____

VENDEE: _____

_____

Appendix C

Books for Real Estate Investors

Landlording: A Handy Manual for Scrupulous Landlords and Landladies Who Do It Themselves, by Leigh Robinson

Home Improvement 1-2-3, by The Home Depot

Investing in Real Estate with Lease Options and "Subject-to" Deals, by Wendy Patton

Investing in Fixer-Uppers, by Jay P. DeCima

Investing in Real Estate, by Gary W. Eldred, PhD

The Millionaire Next Door, by Thomas J. Stanley PhD and William D. Danko, PhD

The Real Estate Investor's Guide to Corporations, LLCs, and Asset Protection Entities, by Richard T. Williamson

Index

About the Author

Michael E. Heeney owns and operates nearly $6 million in income property holdings. He began his career as a salesman but soon enough realized the benefits of investing in real estate. Starting from scratch and learning mostly by trial and error, he persevered and eventually achieved financial independence. *Big Profits from Small Properties* is his first book.

27541527R00137

Made in the USA
Lexington, KY
13 November 2013